Teaching Writing With Picture Books as Models

Lessons and Strategies for Using the
Power of Picture Books to Teach the Elements
of Great Writing in the Upper Grades

by Rosanne Kurstedt and Maria Koutras

SCHOLASTIC
PROFESSIONAL BOOKS

New York • Toronto • London • Auckland • Sydney

Dedications

For my son Jacob, who has showed me the "Wow!" in everyday things. —RK

For my mother, whose life inspires me every day, and whose laughter I still hear in my memories. —MK

Acknowledgements

We know this book would never have happened if it were not for the support and encouragement of so many people. First and foremost, we must thank Denise Levine and Hindy List—Denise for her never-ending love for children and her unselfish, unwavering support and guidance, and Hindy for her unyielding enthusiasm for teaching and learning, and specifically for being the impetus that brought us to Scholastic. We thank Scholastic, particularly Terry Cooper and Wendy Murray for believing that this idea was worth pursuing; and our editor, Joanna Davis-Swing, who so calmly put up with all of our first-time jitters and anxious questions. Thanks also to Adele Schroeter for thoughtfully reading and responding to the manuscript.

We'd like to thank Barbara Schneider for her trust, guidance, and encouragement and for bringing the two of us together. We must thank District 2 for providing the type of community that supports learning, staff development, and professional conversations. And, of course, our students—we'd like to thank all the children who have passed through our classrooms, each one motivating us to strengthen our practice and continue our learning.

Lastly, we'd like to thank our families for their unwavering support and love that has carried us through this process. We love you.

Thanks to the students whose work appears in this book:
Eva Hoffmann, Jonah Miller, Lisa Young, Casey Freedman, Zak Kampton, Thomas Block, Adam Gonzalez, Natalie Meltzer, Margaret Knoerzer, Cary Stathopoulos, Fionna Kenny, Francesca Martinelli, Elli Marcus, Jared Greenfield, Isabella Rieke, Lucy McWhorter Rosen, and Richard Zheng.

Front cover design by Kathy Massaro
Interior design by Sydney Wright
Interior photographs on pages 4, 15, 19, 20, 42, 55, and 72 by Vicky Kasala.
All others courtesy of the authors.
ISBN 0-439-13516-8

Contents

Introduction

▲ *Rosanne reads aloud a picture book during the first week of school.*

My grandfather's barn is sweet-smelling and dark and cool; leather harnesses hang like paintings against old wood; and hay dust floats like gold in the air. Grandfather once lived in the city; and once he lived by the sea; but the barn is the place he loves most. Where else, he says, can the soft sound of cows chewing make all the difference in the world?

—from *All the Places to Love* by Patricia MacLachlan

Reading aloud Patricia MacLachlan's *All the Places to Love* on the first day of school leaves our students speechless. The silent moment reassures us of the awe picture books inspire. The discussion that follows begins our yearlong exploration of writing. After several weeks of reading aloud and talking about picture books, our students aspire to be writers who craft beautiful stories like their favorite authors do—Patricia MacLachlan, Byrd Baylor, Patricia Palocco, Jane Yolen, Chris Van Allsburg, Libba Moore Gray, and Bill Martin Jr.

As teachers, we grapple with the difficult task of teaching students the art and craft of writing. We struggle not only to engage students' interest and motivate them to read widely and critically, but also to help them apply what they've learned about writing and the elements of story to their own work. We have found that using picture books with our upper graders does just this.

The rich language and beautiful rhythm of picture books make them excellent choices for introducing the characteristics of great writing. The short, high-interest stories give students powerful models for learning about building a character, creating a mood, developing a plot, and using sensory details effectively. Students can more easily understand and appreciate how literary elements work from a short, complete work than they can from longer chapter books and novels. (Though we continually reinforce our picture book lessons by recommending that students look for these same elements in their independent novel reading.) Most important, the books motivate students to emulate beautifully crafted language—students eagerly experiment with the techniques and strategies their picture book mentors use with such success.

While some teachers may shy away from the idea of using picture books in their upper-grade classrooms, Thomas Newkirk in *Beyond Words* reminds us, "There are good pragmatic reasons for not packing picture books away after second grade. Even if children shift their reading to longer chapter books, their writing does not expand in this exponential way. . . . The texts children write are more likely to resemble the texts of picture books than longer books composed of extended chapters. Whatever their reading preferences, they will need the picture books as models for their writing" (1992). Picture books remain an immense aid to young writers; as Susan Benedict states in *Beyond Words*, "The length, complexity of story lines and variety (of topics) make them an ideal model for young student writers" (1992). Picture books are a necessary component of an upper-grade library, but certainly they must be balanced with a wide range of books and other reading materials to suit the reading needs and interests of all students.

Ideally, your classroom would be filled with picture books, but if you are just starting out, that is quite unlikely. No matter. The writing techniques and lessons from this book can be successful with just a few well-loved and carefully chosen picture books. We like to call those books we return to over and over our "pinch hitters." We know we can always count on these special books to offer students new insights on writing.

About Us

We teach at a small public school in Manhattan's District 2. The school has two classes each in grades K–5, with one special education class; the population is diverse, attracting students from all over our district and city. Our school embraces a student-centered, inquiry approach to learning that is reflected in all our lessons. We encourage students to ask questions and search for answers, generating their own learning in the process.

Our Classrooms

Our philosophy of teaching and learning is reflected in how we arrange our classrooms. Since we want to foster a sense of community and promote student-centered learning, we reserve a large space for our class meeting area. We scatter tables or clusters of desks around the outer edges of this meeting space where students do their individual and small-group work. This setup gives the room a spacious feel; it isn't cluttered with desks and chairs, and we all have room to move about. We have found students are more engaged in this type of environment, mainly because they can work in a variety of ways. Some choose to sit at the tables while others lean on benches or lie on the floor. The students have more space to work since they aren't confined to desks. This setup also fosters student-to-student talk and encourages students to take responsibility for their learning.

▲ *We arrange our classrooms so students can work efficiently and comfortably.*

The supplies students need (pens, sticky-notes, loose-leaf paper, etc.) are all well organized and easily accessible in the class supply area. Since we allow students access to supplies whenever they need them, and we depend on students to keep the supply area neat and stocked, this arrangement serves to build independence and responsibility. Our classroom library is spread throughout the room, organized in baskets by genre, theme, author, award winners, etc. This way, students can easily select and transport books in their area of interest or study. Again, students play an important role in maintaining organization in the room because they are responsible for returning books to the appropriate basket and making sure the baskets are easy to find.

▲ *We organize our class library in labeled baskets.*

The room arrangement supports our management and lesson flow. All of our lessons begin in the main meeting area with students sitting in a circle on a rug; we've found this encourages better discussions as well as a sense of community. When we read aloud or write on a chart, we usually sit in chairs so students can see better. However, when we're engaged in a discussion with students, we're on their level, kneeling by their desks or sitting on the floor. While this arrangement works for us, your room doesn't have to be laid out the same way for these lessons to succeed. Arrange your room to suit your style and needs, incorporate picture books into your writing curriculum, and get ready for a wonderful year.

Our Writing Program

Our multifaceted writing program owes much to the writing workshop model of Donald Graves and Lucy Calkins. In *The Art of Teaching Writing*, Calkins divides the writing workshop into three phases:

Mini-lesson—a short lesson that teaches a specific idea or strategy and often uses literature or students' own writing as models.

Writing and conferring—students write and the teacher confers with students. Students may also confer with one another.

Share—students share their writing with the class, in small groups or in pairs.

These components are flexible. The share or mini-lesson can be dropped or switched in order according to the day's needs; however, quiet writing and conferring are necessary in every writing lesson (Calkins, 1994, pp. 189–190).

The Writing Process

We organize our workshop into writing cycles. Each cycle explores a different genre and culminates with a published piece, a draft that has gone through all stages of the writing process and is ready to be made public. The process students move through for each cycle is the same and is outlined below; we thank Amy Ludwig of the Teacher's College Reading and Writing Project for introducing us to this process. Notice the emphasis on exploring ideas and topics before drafting begins; the investment of time in this stage of the writing process pays off because kids take the time to discover topics that are meaningful to them and about which they have plenty to say.

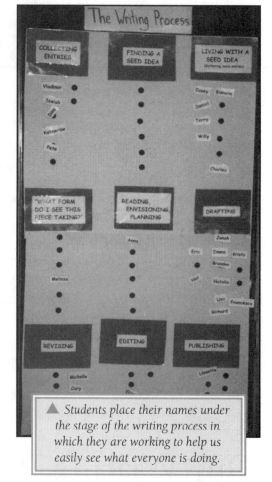

▲ *Students place their names under the stage of the writing process in which they are working to help us easily see what everyone is doing.*

Collecting Entries—Students observe and write about the world around them. We encourage them to write a variety of entries, including what makes them angry, sad, or amazed; overheard conversations; their fears, dreams, or wonderings; and memories. Sometimes we assign them topics to write about, and they also practice writing strategies we've discussed in class. All this writing occurs in students' writer's notebooks.

Finding a Seed—Students choose something from their entries that they want to linger over, something meaningful they are willing to invest time on and develop into a finished piece.

Nurturing a Seed—Students explore their chosen seed idea, writing about the idea from several different angles and homing in on what they really want to say—finding the essence of the piece. Students may also explore the genre of the piece. Students are still writing in their writer's notebooks during this stage.

Drafting—Students draft their pieces outside of their writer's notebooks, drawing upon the entries they've written. The draft can be a compilation of entries from exploring the seed idea or an offshoot of one or more entries.

Revision—Students rework their piece and revise it for content, style, and purpose.

Editing—Students polish their pieces. Finally, students correct spelling, punctuation, and grammar.

Celebration—Students share their work and make it public, by adding it to a class book, hanging it on a bulletin board, reading aloud to a group of peers or parents—the possibilities for celebrating writing abound.

Here's a sample overview of the writing cycles we might study for the year.

September	Exploring great writing
October	Memoirs
November/ December	Nonfiction: editorials, how-tos, feature articles
January	Free cycle (student choice)
February/ March	Realistic fiction
April	Free cycle (student choice)
May	Poetry
June	Reflection

Writing Workshop Schedule

On the next page is our weekly schedule. Notice that reading-and-writing time occurs consistently every day. Young writers need this predictability so they can begin thinking like writers; since they know they'll be writing every day, they begin to think ahead and plan their writing for the day.

	8:40–9:25	9:25–10:10	10:10–10:55	10:55–11:40	11:40–12:35	12:35–1:20	1:20–2:05	2:05–2:50
Monday	Read Aloud	Reading/ Writing	Writing Workshop	Science	Lunch	Math	Math/SS	Social Studies
Tuesday	Read Aloud	Reading/ Writing	Writing Workshop	Spanish	Lunch	Math	Math/SS	Social Studies
Wednesday	Read Aloud	Reading/ Writing	Writing Workshop	Math	Lunch	Art	Art	Math
Thursday	Read Aloud	Reading/ Writing	Writing Workshop	Social Studies	Lunch	Math	Science	Gym
Friday	Read Aloud	Reading/ Writing	Science	Writing Workshop	Lunch	Math	Spanish	Weekly Wrap-up

10–30 minutes—Mini-lesson (when we read a picture book the mini-lesson could be 30 minutes)
20–30 minutes—Writing/conferring
10–15 minutes—Share

We begin each day with a read-aloud of a novel, short story, or picture book. We value this time because it brings the class together as readers, emphasizes the importance we place on reading, and gives us a chance to introduce lots of great literature to our students.

We also set aside 40 to 60 minutes for writing every day. We usually begin the writing period with a mini-lesson and then send students off to work on their pieces. The mini-lessons depend on students' needs and where they are in the writing process. Some are quick—for instance, how to punctuate dialogue—but others, such as when we use picture books, can be 20 to 30 minutes long. If the mini-lesson does go that long, we shorten the student writing time, shorten or postpone the share, or extend the writing workshop for the day.

Writer's Notebook

Our students keep two notebooks for writing: a writer's notebook and a literature notebook. We believe that if we want our students to be writers, we must help them act and think as writers, so we ask them to keep a notebook especially for capturing their thoughts and ideas and for practicing the writing craft. We think of it as Ralph Fletcher does, and introduce it this way to our students: "[A writer's notebook] gives you a place to write down what makes you angry or sad or amazed, to write down what you noticed and don't want to forget, to record exactly what your grandmother whispered in your ear before she said good-bye for the last time. A writer's notebook gives you a place to live like a writer, not just in school during writing time, but wherever you are, at any time of day" (1996). The entries our students collect in their notebooks are springboards for their published writing pieces.

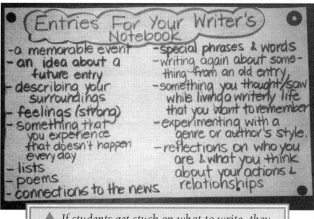

Entries For Your Writer's Notebook
- a memorable event
- an idea about a future entry
- describing your surroundings
- feelings (strong)
- something that you experience that doesn't happen every day
- lists
- poems
- connections to the news
- special phrases & words
- writing again about something from an old entry
- something you thought/saw while living a writerly life that you want to remember
- experimenting with a genre or author's style.
- reflections on who you are & what you think about your actions & relationships

▲ *If students get stuck on what to write, they can check this list of ideas the class created.*

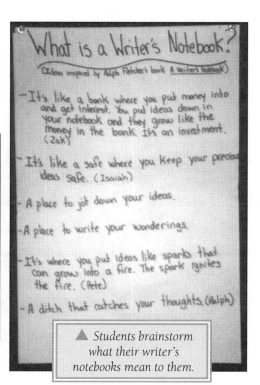

What is a Writer's Notebook?
(Ideas inspired by Ralph Fletcher's book A Writer's Notebook)

- It's like a bank where you put money into and get interest. You put ideas down in your notebook and they grow like the money in the bank. It's an investment. (Zak)

- It's like a safe where you keep your precious ideas safe. (Isaiah)

- A place to jot down your ideas.

- A place to write your wonderings.

- It's where you put ideas like sparks that can grow into a fire. The spark ignites the fire. (Pete)

- A ditch that catches your thoughts. (Ralph)

▲ *Students brainstorm what their writer's notebooks mean to them.*

Literature Notebooks

From the beginning of the year, we emphasize that writer's notebooks are strictly for writing down ideas and thoughts and playing with language. For all other classroom notes and work in reading and writing, we ask students to maintain a five-section notebook, called their literature notebook. We assign each section a name, such as literature responses, vocabulary, mechanics, beautiful language, and words we'd like to use. The sections vary from year to year as we try new ideas, but we always have a writing craft section, which is where students take notes during read-alouds, minilessons, and discussions.

Students use their writer's notebooks and literature notebooks together throughout the year. For example, in the writing craft section of a literature notebook, a student might have the criteria for what makes a great book review. In the writer's notebook, you might find three different beginnings for a book review where the student was practicing and working on various writing techniques.

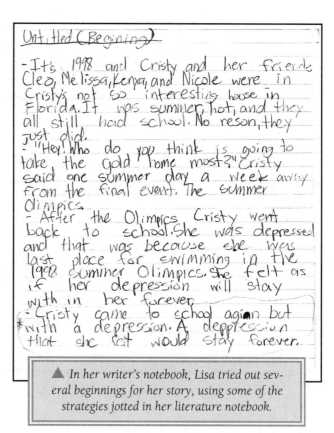

Beginings

- Start with setting.✱
- Start with someone speaking and then get into the setting and story.
- Start telling with facts - details about character
- Anectdote retelling story about the character
- Dialogue
- Start right in with the action
- Start with conflict.
- Introduce the narrator/character like in charlotte
- Use details to set a moode ot Boyle
  get an idea of setting.
- Get a catchy begging so reader will read
- Start with a goute so reader can make predictions.
- Start with the moral.

▲ *Lisa recorded various techniques writers use to begin stories in her literature notebook.*

Untitled (Begining)

- It's 1998 and Cristy and her friends Cleo, Melissa, Kenya, and Nicole were in Cristy's not so interesting house in Florida. It was summer, hot, and they all still had school. No reson, they just did.
- "Hey! Who do you think is going to take the gold home most?" Cristy said one summer day a week away from the final event. The summer Olimpics.
- After the Olimpics, Cristy went back to school. She was depressed and that was because she was last place for swimming in the 1998 summer Olimpics. She felt as if her depression will stay with in her forever.
✱ - Cristy came to school agian but with a depression. A depression that she sat would stay forever.

▲ *In her writer's notebook, Lisa tried out several beginnings for her story, using some of the strategies jotted in her literature notebook.*

Becoming Writers

From the very first day, we try to help our students see themselves as writers. In the first few weeks, our students do a great deal of talking and thinking about writing. They share their writing experiences, discussing when writing worked for them. Sometimes they draw time lines of their writing lives, to highlight their growth and successes as writers. We often share pieces of our own writing, discussing a paper we wrote for a professor and the difficulties we faced. We have even brought in multiple drafts of this manuscript to show students that all writers go through the writing process. Additionally, we show students our writer's notebooks so they see that writing transcends the boundaries of school and that we understand the difficulties they might face because we keep writer's notebooks, too. Our students smile from ear to ear when we share pieces of our writing lives with them. They feel special and important because we share our experiences, thereby including them in our lives.

Another way to create a community of writers is to immerse students in exciting literature. We do this through our daily read-alouds, buddy reading, and independent reading time. Students then have a common body of literature to discuss and draw upon in their own writing efforts.
We also maintain charts on the writing strategies we talk about in class.

We revisit, discuss, and update the charts throughout the year; they hang in the classroom and students copy them in their notebooks. They capture students' knowledge, record their growth as writers, and provide a common link among students. Some charts we use every year include WORDS WE LOVE, GREAT DESCRIPTIONS, and IDEAS FOR WRITING. Since students generated the charts, they feel a sense of ownership toward them and refer to them during writing time.

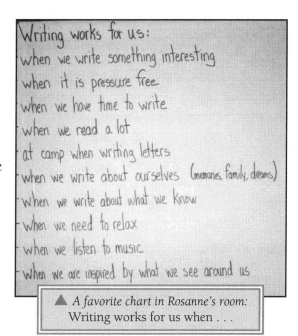

Writing works for us:
when we write something interesting
when it is pressure free
when we have time to write
when we read a lot
at camp when writing letters
when we write about ourselves (memories, family, dreams)
when we write about what we know
when we need to relax
when we listen to music
when we are inspired by what we see around us

▲ *A favorite chart in Rosanne's room:* Writing works for us when . . .

Recommended READING

Below is a list of professional books we use at the beginning of the year.

What a Writer Needs by Ralph Fletcher

A Writer's Notebook by Ralph Fletcher

Writing Towards Home by Georgia Heard

In the Middle by Nancie Atwell

Wondrous Words by Katie Wood Ray

Integrating Writing Into the Classroom

In addition to the pieces students publish from their writer's notebooks, our students publish monthly book reviews and social studies reports (which take many forms, such as narrative accounts, newspapers, calendars, and brochures). Students incorporate what they learn during writing workshop into these pieces, too. Throughout this book, we mention which lessons apply to nonfiction writing—including great beginnings, strong endings, and voice.

What You Will Find In This Book

In this book you will find lessons, conversations, student work, and class charts that illuminate how picture books can enhance any writing program. We've included extensive picture book lists at the beginning of each chapter, sharing those we find most helpful for teaching specific writing techniques. In Chapter 1, we outline how we use picture books to teach writing elements to upper graders, while Chapter 2 highlights the writing strategies and lessons we address early in the year and revisit again and again, including memorable language, strong verbs, and sensory detail.

Chapter 3 describes memoir writing, which is usually our first writing cycle of the year. Chapter 4 covers mood, voice, and point of view, elements that apply to all genres and that we generally teach in conjunction with our first writing cycle and revisit throughout the year.

Chapters 5 describes how we teach realistic fiction. The lessons in this chapter guide you through the planning and drafting stages of the writing process. We discuss character, theme, and plot in the context of the students' emerging stories.

Chapters 6 through 8 present lessons we use during the revision stage of the writing process, including creating strong beginnings and endings, using time effectively, and incorporating monologue and dialogue.

You can use the lessons in this book sequentially, but we recommend that you adapt the ideas to your own and your class's needs—as we do every year. After all, learning how to write isn't a linear process, and our classrooms reflect that. Throughout the year, we revisit specific writing strategies or genres based on the needs of our students. Thus, we are continually reinforcing skills that have been taught in previous lessons. Follow the sequence you feel is appropriate for your students, and do not hesitate to backtrack or repeat. That is all part of the teaching and learning process.

Our classroom environments are places where students experiment with their writing and stretch their thinking. We expose our students to good writing and establish our expectations that this is a place to learn, practice, question, and lead a writerly life.

In the past few years, we have witnessed a transformation in our students' writing, and we attribute a great deal of their growth to our use of picture books as models. We invite you to take a look at what we're doing so you too can empower your students and help them become practicing writers.

CHAPTER 1

▲ *Students peruse a picture book to get ideas for a writer's notebook entry.*

Using Picture Books as Writing Models

When we first sit down with a picture book, we get lost in the story. We look at the pictures, we focus on the events, and we identify with the main character. We may notice the beautiful language, but our enjoyment of the story stems primarily from the developing plot. We are readers, and that's what readers do.

As Katie Wood Ray points out in *Wondrous Words*, inviting students to read a story as writers helps them learn about the craft of writing from the experts. This process asks students to see with different eyes, to notice voice, mood, and metaphors, much as a carpenter or architect might walk into a house and appreciate its fine structure. Writers look beyond the plot and notice the craft, the way the story is designed and built. "Reading like writers" is a skill that must be taught and practiced in the classroom.

To help our students learn to read as writers, we must first encourage them to read widely and to think of themselves as writers. That is why we use picture books as our initial texts for exploring writing. We read them aloud, make them available during independent reading time, and often conduct a picture book mini-inquiry (described later in this chapter) early in the year. When students are familiar with the story lines, the characters, and the settings of books, they are able to distance themselves from the plot and focus on the writing. With your support and guidance, students will begin to read all texts more critically, applying their writer's eyes to the authors' craft.

Of course, this shift from reading for story to reading as writer takes time and practice. We begin on the very first day of school by reading a picture book aloud and asking open-ended questions such as, *What did you notice? Which images linger in your mind?* We make connections in our daily read-aloud discussion to the work we do during writing workshop. We reread books, prodding students to delve further into their understanding of the story, to notice the subtle, yet clever, decisions the author has made. Then we provide many opportunities for students to practice the techniques they notice in their own work.

Rereading a text and noticing the craft is similar to what a basketball coach does the day after a game. He or she rewinds the videotape of the game and watches it over and over again, carefully observing all the plays and choosing those worth emulating. Then the coach can show the tape to players, stopping at specific points to highlight exactly what the team will practice before the next game. We guide our students through lessons and activities that use picture books to illustrate the craft of writing and help them apply literary techniques to their own work, coaching their writing moves as they take their shot at using metaphor or setting a mood.

Overview of a Picture Book Lesson

All of our picture book–based writing lessons have a similar format. We read and reread picture books a number of times for multiple purposes, focusing attention on a different literary element each time. Ideally, students should be familiar with a picture book before you use it as a teaching tool; that way, they can focus on the purpose of the lesson and not worry about following the events of the story. Because of time constraints and programming issues, we sometimes do not have this luxury. This is okay. You can give summaries of stories before you read them, and remember to revisit old favorites for new lessons.

Following the same format provides a consistency and predictability that is helpful for our students. The components of each lesson are

* Introduction
* Focus for Discussion
* Reading of the Picture Book
* Try It Out

* Conferring
* Class Share
* Homework

For space considerations, we have not included each component for each lesson in the book, but the following descriptions will give you a sense of how each part would go.

✓ Introduction

We begin each lesson with an overview of its purpose, being sure to establish a connection with the students and their work. For instance, Rosanne might preface a lesson with, "We have been studying the language authors use to describe, and we have begun to borrow their techniques and use them in our own writing. We're working on choosing details that will help readers see setting and characters more vividly. I've noticed that some of you have been struggling with this, so I thought it would be a good idea to look at some more models. I chose *Island Summer* by Catherine Stock, since I think she does a wonderful job of creating images. Let's read the title and look at the cover. What kind of images do you think she might create in this book?"

✓ Focus for Listening

After introducing the book and the purpose of the lesson, we assign students a listening task. This "focus for listening" is directly related to the purpose of the lesson. For example, if we're studying descriptive language, we may ask the students to pay close attention to how and when the author uses description in the book. Students take notes in their literature notebooks. If the students are not familiar with the

▲ *Students follow along during a read-aloud.*

book, giving them a brief summary beforehand allows them to focus on the listening task while enjoying the story.

We ask our students to take notes as soon as they have their literature notebooks, which is usually the second week of school. Since we know our students received note-taking instruction in the fourth grade (in preparation for standardized tests), we are confident that they have basic skills in this area. However, we do check to see if they're having trouble, and we consistently model note taking on the overhead and on chart paper. The first few times we ask our students to take notes, we pay close attention to how they respond. Are they constantly writing? Are they interrupting the read-aloud to say, "I missed that"? Are they even attempting to take notes? Based on these informal assessments, we can get a feel for who is effectively taking notes and who needs some practice.

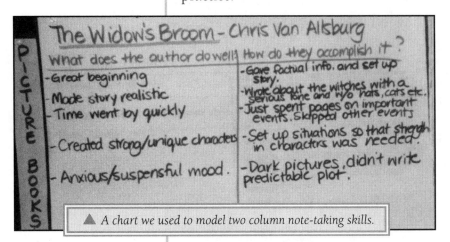

▲ A chart we used to model two column note-taking skills.

If your students haven't received instruction in note taking before, you'll probably want to spend several sessions discussing and modeling note-taking skills. We work on note taking throughout the year in all subject areas. Before our read-alouds, we prepare charts to help our students organize their notes. We explain an efficient way for students to divide up their pages by making charts in their own notebooks. Here are a few ideas that might help you teach the note-taking skills your students need.

* Use the overhead regularly to model note taking.
* Discuss note-taking criteria (jotting key phrases, noting main idea, etc.).
* Read aloud excerpts of stories or books and have students practice jotting down notes.
* Have students read excerpts and practice note taking.
* Have students compare notes with partners.
* Use the overhead to share some student strategies and their notes after a read-aloud.
* Record strategies on a chart and add to it as new strategies are modeled or discovered.

✓ Discussion

After we read the picture book aloud, we begin a discussion with an open-ended question such as, "What did you notice?" or "What do you think?" We encourage students to support their ideas with the story, grounding the discussion in the text. We try to have the students lead the conversation, not us. This practice is very important. It is also very difficult to implement. Most students are so used to teacher-kid-teacher dialogue that they need coaching to carry on conversations among themselves. The effort is worth it; when students are directing their own learning, it becomes more meaningful and students are more invested in their work.

Occasionally, discussions lose their focus. If this happens, we intervene by reiterating the lesson's purpose or summarizing how what has been said relates to the purpose of the discussion. Sometimes students propose an insightful and important idea that simply isn't relevant to the day's lesson; we validate the idea and suggest that we should think about it over the next few days and revisit it with our full attention. We're sure to follow through, to keep our word, and to encourage our students to be risk takers with their ideas and insights.

As mentioned above, during discussions, we always make it a point to ask students to support their ideas with evidence from the text. When students offer ideas, we can say things like:

* *How did the author let you know that?*
* *What in the story gave you that impression?*
* *Can you show us where in the story you noticed that?*

We've found that if we consistently model rereading parts of the text to support ideas, students soon learn to do it on their own.

▲ *Maria writes notes on a Venn diagram based on the classroom discussion.*

✓ Try It Out

After the discussion, we review the writing strategy or technique we'd like them to try out during that day's writing time. To smooth the transition into a focused and productive independent work time, we allow a couple of minutes for students to collect their thoughts. Sometimes we have them talk to a partner about their ideas or jot down notes for themselves in their writer's notebooks. Often we ask them to give the strategy a brief try before moving off to work independently. After those few minutes, we ask a few students to share their plans. This "thinking and sharing" helps focus students and gives those who are stuck some ideas. We stay at the rug and create a small circle with students who need more explanation of the lesson or the assignment, while others move quietly to their work areas.

TIP BOX

Sometimes students are not ready to practice the writing technique we discuss in the mini-lesson. They may not be at that point of the writing process in their current piece, or they may have a plan that is working well for them and not want to be interrupted. This is okay, and we allow students to work on their plan if they're in the thick of things. Everyone has been introduced to the topic and can revisit it whenever appropriate.

✓ Conferring

While the class is working, we go around the room and have brief (two- to five-minute) conferences with individual students. We may start the conference with a general question such as, "How's it going?" Depending on the student's response, we ask clarifying and probing questions to get more information, or make suggestions to move the student along. If we notice that many students are having the same difficulty or are confused, we try to clarify the assignment. We often plan future mini-lessons based on what we see happening in conference. Sometimes we ask a student to share what he or she has done with the class during our share time. After all, share time is a great opportunity to highlight a strategy a student is using successfully.

✓ Class Share

We always bring the class back together to share what students have done. Based on what we were discussing in the day's lesson and what we noticed during conferences, we may ask particular students to read their work and discuss the strategies they used or the

▲ *Rosanne confers with a student during writing time.*

problems they encountered. This is another great opportunity for student-to-student talk, where they can ask each other questions, make suggestions, and learn from one another.

✓ Homework

At the end of the lesson, we give homework that is a continuation of, or directly related to, what we did in class. Assignments vary depending on where in the writing process students are. For example, if they're collecting entries or practicing a specific strategy, we might ask them to write two pages a night.

Picture Book Mini-Inquiries

A few times a year we plan picture book mini-inquiries, a series of picture book lessons that focus intensely and extensively on a specific writing technique or genre. During these inquiries, which last several weeks, we immerse students in picture books and encourage them to read and reread them with a critical eye. This process gives students extra practice "reading as writers," provides opportunities for student-to-student talk, and helps students see picture book authors as writing mentors they can turn to again and again. A mini-inquiry generally digs deeper into a topic than a picture book lesson and involves many picture books rather than just one. For instance, if we are studying leads, a picture book lesson would allow us to read and discuss how one author crafted an introduction to one book. A mini-inquiry, on the other hand, would enable students to read and reread lots of picture books and study a variety of leads, drawing their own conclusions about the kinds of leads possible and when particular strategies are appropriate.

Defining a Purpose

The first time Maria conducted a picture book mini-inquiry in her classroom, it was to explore picture books as a genre. At the time she was turning to picture books for their wonderful writing, and she wanted her students to work on creating picture books of their own. Unexpectedly and fortuitously, the study became bigger than she had ever imagined. Her students discovered that picture books were written in a variety of genres and contained multiple examples of beautifully crafted characters, scenes, and stories. The possibilities for exploration seemed endless, and her students

TIP BOX

Using typed transcripts of a text actually has some unique advantages. For one, it allows you to use a book as a model without having to search for or buy copies. It enables students to underline parts that they notice and even write in the margins. Be sure to type text precisely as it is written; indicate page breaks and include all punctuation, since authors break text and punctuate purposefully. Keeping a file of the typed texts in your classroom also encourages students to revisit the texts when needed and to take copies home. Remember to get the publisher's permission first.

spent weeks exploring various facets of picture books—but they spent very little time writing on their own. Although they were reading and discussing literature critically, they were not applying what they learned to their own work, so Maria decided to rethink her approach.

Maria's mini-inquiries now don't attempt to pursue something as broad as picture books as a genre. Instead, she chooses a literary element or technique to concentrate on—dialogue or leads, for instance—gathers books with great examples of the element or technique, and invites students to dive in and study the craft decisions authors make. She then asks students to examine their own work in light of what they've learned, and practice the techniques they discover.

Choosing and Gathering Books

The books you choose will depend on the purpose of the mini-inquiry. Throughout the years, we have noticed that there are some books we turn to over and over again for a variety of purposes—you will see these books referred to frequently in the following chapters: *Owl Moon, An Angel for Solomon Singer, All the Places to Love,* and *Amos & Boris,* to name just a few. We know these books so well that we can almost recite them from memory. While that is certainly not a prerequisite, it is important to know a book well before you introduce it for a picture book inquiry, so you are sure it fits your lesson's purpose and you have some ideas for guiding students in case they get stuck. The book lists in this book will help you get started, but soon you'll discover your own favorites.

Once you've chosen the books to suit your purpose, you must gather enough copies; this can be a challenging task. Typically, our students work in groups of four or five, and we try to find enough titles to allow each group to work with a different book, and for each group member to have a copy. We usually have six groups in a class, so we need four or five copies of six different books, at a minimum. We scour other classroom libraries, school and local libraries, and send letters home with a list of needed titles, hoping to get some donations or loans from families. Even with your best efforts, you may not find all the copies you are looking for. An alternative that we have found equally as effective is typing up the text and providing one copy of the book for the group to use together.

Planning the Lessons and Activities

Once we've decided on our lesson's purpose and chosen our picture books, we think about the structure of our inquiry. We usually spend the

A group works from a typewritten transcript of a picture book.

first few days reading and rereading aloud the books we've chosen. We read the books the groups will focus on, as well as other books that we feel serve our lesson's objective—this is a good way to use a book you love but can't get enough copies of. We often read excerpts from longer texts and from a variety of other sources, such as magazines, other students' writing (with their permission), or our own writing, if it's appropriate.

After immersing students for a few days in literature and talking about what they notice, the structure of the lesson changes. We still begin with a read-aloud, but now after reading and discussing one book as a class, we ask groups to work together on their own books. We come together at the end of class to share what the groups have learned. Assigned writing activities then help students put into practice the writing techniques they notice during class.

Depending on the purpose of your mini-inquiry, you may guide discussions by providing prompts or questions, or you may let students generate their own queries. Groups may work with the same book throughout the study, or they may change books each week. The specific lessons and activities you choose will depend on the initial sessions of the study, when you learn what your students know, what they need to learn, and what they're interested in.

Although there are many variables to consider, picture book mini-inquiries are most powerful when they are well planned, when they have a specific purpose, and when the right books are explored. As the year progresses and we read more and more books and build our common repertoire, it becomes increasingly natural for students to turn to these authors as mentors—which is the ultimate purpose of a picture book inquiry.

CHAPTER 2

▲ *A sixth grader reads a picture book, searching for memorable language.*

Recognizing Memorable Language and Other Introductory Lessons

O ur students are hooked on picture books from the very first read-aloud. We build on their enthusiasm by talking together about the stories we read, drawing out precisely what it is that makes the stories appealing to them. In this way, the class starts to discuss writing techniques; we develop a common vocabulary and a repertoire of shared stories to draw on throughout the year. This chapter highlights several introductory lessons we like to teach at the beginning of the year.

Memorable Language

An easy way to get students talking about literature is to ask them to listen for *memorable language*. This term is nonthreatening and allows students to point out what they like in a story without having to give it a label.

Sample Lesson on Memorable Language

Rosanne often chooses Jane Yolen's *Owl Moon* to begin a discussion of memorable language. Its beautiful language, rich with sensory details, makes it a good choice for a first discussion of literary techniques. Rosanne prepares a chart template beforehand that helps to focus the discussion; during class, she will fill it in with students' responses. The template is shown below.

Memorable Language
Owl Moon by Jane Yolen

Memorable Lines   What is she doing?

✓ Focus for Listening

Rosanne: While I read *Owl Moon* by Jane Yolen, I want you to pay close attention to her writing. What words and images stand out for you? What about her use of language do you particularly like?

As Rosanne reads, students jot notes to themselves to remind them of the parts they want to share with the class.

✓ Discussion

Rosanne: We'll keep track of everything on this chart [points to chart]. Okay, what did you notice? Carrie?

Carrie: The author, I mean Jane Yolen, describes the setting a lot with colors. Like when she says *black shadows*, *black trees*, and *white snow*.

Havier: Yeah, in the beginning the whole first page was her describing the woods. And about a train whistling [looks in his notebook] like a *sad, sad song*. It makes you feel like you're there. She does a lot with sound. She goes

Recommended READING

All the Places to Love by Patricia MacLachlan

All Those Secrets of the World by Jane Yolen

Fireflies! by Julie Brinckloe

Grandpa's Face by Eloise Greenfield

Harlem by Walter Dean Myers

Home Place by Crescent Dragonwagon

I'm in Charge of Celebrations by Byrd Baylor

Jumanji by Chris Van Allsburg

Letting Swift River Go by Jane Yolen

Lotus Seed by Sherry Garland

Midnight in the Mountains by Julie Lawson

My Mama Had a Dancing Heart by Libba Moore Gray

Nothing Ever Happens on 90th Street by Roni Schotter

Owl Moon by Jane Yolen

Patricia Polacco Books

Sky Tree by Thomas Locker

The Memory Box by Mary Kay Shanley

The Relatives Came by Cynthia Rylant

The Seashore Book by Charlotte Zolotow

When I Go Camping with Grandma by Marion Dane Bauer

Water Dance by Thomas Locker

William Steig Books

back to the trains in the second page too, with the dogs, and she writes how the owls and the father speak to each other with the *whooing*.

Rosanne: Does anyone know what you call that, when you use a word that sounds like the actual sound? [Pauses.] It's called *onomatopoeia*. Did you have something to add, Natasha?

Natasha: She describes a lot of stuff with interesting words like . . . *crunched*, *stained*, and *threading*. I think she is pretty good at that.

Luke: She does stuff like that a lot; sometimes it's not even the word she uses but the picture she describes.

Carrie: Yeah, like the owl pumping his wings— I could feel the power of the owl and see him flying away.

Natasha: You know, most of the words we're talking about are verbs: *pumped*, *crunched*. That's neat.

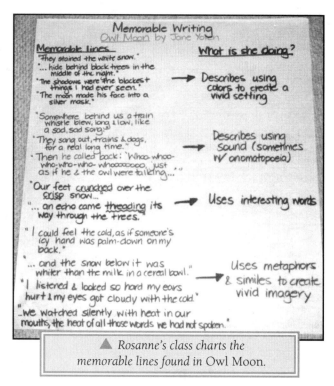

▲ *Rosanne's class charts the memorable lines found in Owl Moon.*

Rosanne: Good point, Natasha. What else did you notice?

Luke: She talks about the boy being cold and says that it is like someone putting a cold hand down the boy's back.

Havier: Yeah, I could almost feel that.

Rosanne: Here, let's find that spot: "I could feel the cold, as if someone's icy hand was palm-down on my back."

Ahmad: There's another part, too—when she says the snow was whiter than the milk in a cereal bowl.

Denise: She also mentions about how he listens so hard that his ears hurt and looked so hard that his eyes got blurry.

Rosanne: [Turning to the page] "I listened and looked so hard my ears hurt and my eyes got cloudy with the cold."

Kathy: [Looks in her notebook] And she writes how the heat from their mouths was like words not spoken. Something like that.

Rosanne: Oh yeah, that's one of my favorite lines. [Finds the page.] "We watched silently with heat in our mouths, the heat of all those words we had not spoken." Yes, that's a great image. To wrap up, why do you think I love this book and chose to read it?

Havier: Because the language flows and it sounds poetic.

Jane: She also uses great words, not ordinary words.

Kenny: Well, actually, she sometimes uses ordinary words. I think it's how she puts them together.

Denise: I think she was great at describing things, like the setting.

Rosanne: Great. So using colors and sounds, choosing strong verbs, and creating images are some of the things authors do to keep us interested.

As you can glean from this conversation, our aim is to heighten students' awareness of what elements contribute to memorable writing, encouraging them to "read like writers." In keeping with this mind-set, we consistently ask students to return to the text to support their ideas.

✓ Try It Out

After the discussion, Rosanne invites students to spend 20 minutes looking through picture books in the class library, paying particular attention to the language the writers chose and the strategies they used to create images. When they have found something memorable, students jot it in their note-books to prepare for a share we will have the next day. They continue their study for homework, with each student taking home one picture book.

Amos + Boris William Steig
"They knew they might never meet again. They knew they would never forget each other"

My Mama had a Dancing Heart Libba Moore Gray
"My mama had a dancing heart and she shared that heart with me."

All those secrets of the World Jane Yolen
"We whirled around and around
under the whispering sycamores
until neither one of us
could tell big from little,
young from old,
short from long,
peace from war,
all those secrets of the world."

When I was young in the Mountains Cythnia Ryiant
When I was young in the mountains,
I never wanted to go to the ocean, and I never wanted to go to the desert. I never wanted to go anywhere else in the world, for I was in mountains. And that was always enough.

▲ *Memorable language recorded
in one student's writing notebook.*

We also ask them to be on the lookout for memorable writing in their independent reading—we encourage them to use sticky-notes to mark the memorable language in their chapter books and bring them to the class share as well.

Exploring Where Ideas Come From

As part of our continuing discussion of what makes a great story, we talk about how writers get their ideas. We like to do a lesson on this topic early in the year, so our students have tools at their fingertips when we first invite them to write their own stories and they are faced with a blank page.

Other "Finding Ideas" Lessons

Throughout the year, we generate ways to help students discover compelling content. Other lessons we've used successfully:

❋ We have students brainstorm a list of topics they're interested in, in their writer's notebooks; they can then refer to their list when they are searching for writing ideas. We've also found it helpful to compile the individual lists into a giant class-idea list, which we post in the room.

❋ We brainstorm topics as a class on a chart to help guide students to write about things they know and things that matter to them. Some topics classes have come up with are pets, siblings, grandparents, vacation spots, and friends.

❋ We brainstorm a list of possible writing genres such as memoirs, narratives, letters, articles, poetry, or responses to literature/news/movies, and display the chart.

❋ We read excerpts from *A Writer's Notebook* by Ralph Fletcher, *Writing Toward Home* by Georgia Heard, *What a Writer Needs* by Ralph Fletcher, and *Hey World, Here I Am!*, by Jean Little.

❋ We write in front of students (modeling), so they can see us thinking through such issues as finding an idea, describing something with the senses, or using memorable language.

❋ We take students through our writer's notebooks to show them entries and think aloud about how to turn entries into topics.

Sample Lesson on Where Ideas Come From

A book that addresses the problem of what to write about is *Nothing Ever Happens on 90th Street* by Roni Schotter. A young girl named Eva has a writing assignment for homework, and she is stuck. She asks her neighbors for help and receives some wonderful advice from this eccentric bunch. Students love this story; they can relate to Eva's dilemma, and they get some clever ideas and helpful strategies to use for themselves.

Book Excerpt:

Nothing Ever Happens on 90th Street

Here are some of the helpful hints Eva receives from her neighbors:

The actor, Mr. Sims, suggests "Watch the stage carefully, observe the players carefully, and don't neglect the details."

The baker, Mr. Morley, says, "Try to find the poetry in your pudding . . .. There's always a new way with old words."

The ballerina, Alexis, tells Eva to "use her imagination . . . stretch the truth . . . ask what if?"

Mrs. Maritinez suggests Eva "Add a little action . . .. A little of this. A little of that. And don't forget the spice. Mix it. Stir it. Make something happen. Surprise yourself!"

✓ Introduction

Rosanne: Today we will be reading *Nothing Ever Happens on 90th Street* by Roni Schotter. As you know, we have been talking and thinking a lot about writing. I think this book will help us with some things we've been working on. Let's see. In this book a little girl has a homework assignment to write. In the beginning she has nothing to write about and is frustrated. Has that ever happened to any of you?

Some students nod yes.

Rosanne: Well, what did you do?

Steven: I asked a friend for some ideas.

Alice: If it's homework, I sometimes ask my mom or dad.

✓ Focus for Listening

Rosanne: That's great. Maybe we'll all get some more ideas from this book. I want you to listen really closely for what strategies she learns that help her to write her homework assignment. Afterward, we'll have a discussion and chart what we find.

Rosanne reads aloud the book.

✓ Discussion

Rosanne: Take a few moments to think about what Eva learns. [Pauses.] What writing strategies do you think she learns?

Jason: Well, she definitely got help from her friends and other people.

Rosanne: She certainly did. But what specifically did they tell her? How did they help?

Alice: The dancer told her to stretch the truth and use her imagination.

Kenny: She also said to ask "What if?"

Rosanne: Okay, I'll write those two things on the chart. Anything else?

Karen: Well, in the beginning, someone told her to use details.

Rosanne: Yes, is that all he said? Let's reread that beginning part. [Flips to beginning of the book and reads.]

> "Writing?," he asked. "Trying to," Eva answered, "but nothing ever happens on 90th Street!" "You are mistaken, my dear," Mr. Sims said. "The world's a stage—even 90th Street—and each of us plays a

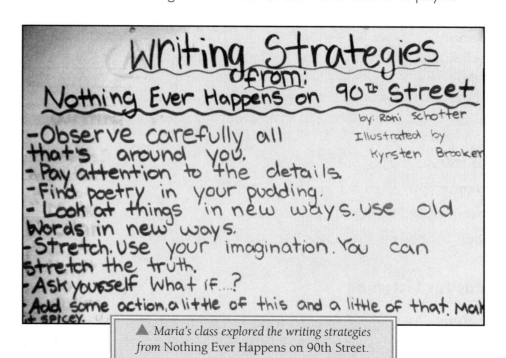

▲ *Maria's class explored the writing strategies from* Nothing Ever Happens on 90th Street.

part. Watch the stage, observe the players carefully, and don't neglect the details," he said.

Okay, so what is Mr. Sims suggesting Eva do?

Karen: Oh, he's saying to watch carefully, and don't forget the details.

Alice: Also to look around you, because there's lots to write about.

Rosanne: Yes, that's it. I'll write those things down. Anything else?

Carol: The baker said there's "poetry in your pudding." I liked that.

Sam: I don't get that.

Rosanne: I'm glad you asked, good for you! I'm sure you're not the only one who doesn't get it. Does anyone want to explain that?

Kenny: Well, I think he meant to use nice words. Like, in *Owl Moon*, Jane Yolen made it sound like poetry.

Rosanne: Great. Let's read that part again.

"Try to find poetry in your pudding" Mr. Morley said softly. "There's always a new way with old words." "You're right," Eva said, wishing Mr. Morley would one day find the poetry in his pudding. Taking his advice, she tried to think up a new way to describe the look of Mr. Morley's mousse. Smooth and dark as midnight. Or maybe more like mink! Yes, that was it! Eva thought, writing in her notebook.

Kenny: Oh yeah. He said there are new ways at looking at things.

Rosanne: Yes. Does anyone know what "smooth and dark as midnight" is?

Alice: I think it's a simile. It's making a comparison using *like* or *as*.

Rosanne: Right.

Kenny: So that would be a new way of looking at things—if you made a comparison of two things you don't normally think of.

Sam: We should add similes to the list then. And what about metaphors? Aren't those like similes?

Karen: Yeah, except you don't use *like* or *as*.

Rosanne: I'll write down "add poetry to your pudding" by looking at things in new ways, and using similes and metaphors. Does anyone want to say any more about that?

We continue the discussion until the students mention all the strategies that Eva learns. As we always do at the end of a lesson, Rosanne rereads the chart

TIP BOX

In March, Maria's class put together a chart so students could borrow ideas from one another. Students looked through their writer's notebooks and jotted down some of the topics they had written about. They wrote these on little cards and put them into a pocket chart. Students looking for ideas could check out the chart and borrow from other students.

to clarify what was discussed. She also emphasizes that Eva found ideas by writing about what she knew and by observing the world around her. She invites students to write about what they see around them, without neglecting the details. "Write what you see and add a little spice," she says.

✓ Trying It Out

We now ask our students to write in their writer's notebooks for the first time. They are enthusiastic, bubbling with ideas from this lesson and from all the reading, talking, and thinking we've been doing. But before sending students off to write, we ask them to turn to a partner and share three ideas. Then we take a few moments to brainstorm other topics; below is a list generated by a fifth-grade class.

Ideas for Writing

My mother	My twin sister
A book	The classroom
The rug	My summer home
My dog	My cat

This quick idea-fest enables students to get ideas from one another. The students who do not know what they are going to write, even after the share, stay on the rug to confer. While the class is getting settled with their writing, Rosanne meets briefly with these other students. They usually just need a little encouragement or an added explanation of the strategies. When they finish, Rosanne moves about the room, conferring with students.

Sometimes writing time is totally silent. Other times, we may give students time at the beginning or end of writing to confer with peers. Students who want to confer while the class is having quiet writing time can either meet with the teacher or move to a corner of the room and confer quietly with a peer. We emphasize respecting the needs of others for quiet time while acknowledging that talking and peer feedback are also necessary for most writers.

✓ Sample Conference: Highlighting Strengths

As Rosanne walks around the room to confer with those students who'd like to talk, she notices that Jonah has stopped writing, so she sits next to him to see how he is doing.

Rosanne: How's it going?

Jonah: Fine.

▲ *Maria confers with a student.*

Rosanne: What are you writing about?

Jonah: Observing what's around me and noticing the details.

Rosanne: Will you read me what you have so far?

Jonah: *In front of me lies a rug filled with color. It's lined with patterns and designs. It seems dark because the colors are not bright. Red overpowers all other colors by dramatic amounts. Upon the rug lie books, sheets, and folders strewn about, unorganized and filled with lost content. Students sit upon it thinking and writing. Some stare out wondering what to write while others write without stopping to look up for a second.*

Rosanne: That is a great start. I particularly like how you described the way "the work is strewn" about and the writers are searching for ideas. I noticed you've stopped writing.

Jonah: Well, I'm kind of stuck. I don't know what to write next.

Rosanne: Remember when we talked about memorable language in *Owl Moon*?

Jonah: Yeah.

Rosanne: What are some strategies Jane Yolen used?

Jonah: Well, she used sound a lot. Rugs don't make much noise, though. I guess I could use another sense. I've done a lot with what the rug looks like; maybe I can describe what it feels like.

Rosanne: Good idea.

In this conference Rosanne pointed out what Jonah did well, which was describing what the rug looked like. She then helped him choose a specific strategy for making the entry even better by extending the description to how the rug might have felt. This was what Jonah added to his entry: "The warmth of the rug is a nice change from the cold starkness of the floor. It is comforting and plush even though I see old staples and bits of debris tucked inside its little fingers." He also incorporated a new strategy, using figurative language to describe the rug's fabric as *its little fingers*.

✓ Class Share

After the students write for about 20 minutes, Rosanne calls them back to the meeting area. She asks some students with whom she conferred to share.

Rosanne: As I went around the room, I noticed that many of you were using the strategies we've been discussing to help get ideas. I'd like some of you to share what you did, so we can talk about how these strategies work in the real world. Katherine, would you like to get us started?

Katherine: Well, originally, I was going to observe what was around me, and I saw a book. I love books and reading, so I wrote about that. But when I read it over, it didn't sound so great. I didn't like it. Then Rosanne came over, and I decided to try to add "poetry to the pudding." I tried to think of some metaphors and similes so I could describe books in a more interesting way. I like it much better now.

Rosanne: Will you read it for us?

Katherine reads her entry:

Give me an object. My book? Okay. A book is filled with adventure crammed into words, meaning stuffed full. In the binding it has a wonderful story to tell. Books jump out, they yell "pick me, pick me, I'm the right choice, you'll see, you'll see." Reading is the key to unlocking treasure—stories, memories, wishes, inspiration. A book is like a glittering diamond, a golden ring, a favorite bracelet. Writing is to be able to grab words, puzzle pieces, and fit them together to make a whole puzzle that's a complete picture.

Rosanne: Thanks, Katherine. So you decided to observe the world around you, and since books are a big part of our classroom and you like reading, you chose that for your topic. And to write about it in a new way, you came up with some similes and metaphors. Does anyone have any comments?

Jason: I like the metaphors she used, how reading is a key and books are treasures.

Rosanne: Yes, that's nice, isn't it?

Delia: It really shows how valuable she thinks reading is, and how great books can be. I hadn't thought of it that way, and I like the idea of a book being a treasure chest—it makes me think of secrets and pirates and gold and jewels. It makes reading seem adventurous.

Rosanne: Yes. Metaphors are powerful, helping us make new connections. Any other comments?

Mark: She also uses similes to describe books—she says they're like diamonds. It goes along with the metaphor.

Rosanne: It sure does. What else do you notice?

Miguel: She also compares writing to making a puzzle. That was cool. Writing is hard, and it helps to think of it as putting together a puzzle— words are the puzzle pieces that you fit together to make up the idea you want, the picture in the puzzle.

Rosanne: I like that too. What kind of comparison is that?

Delia: I think it's a metaphor because the words are puzzle pieces—a finished piece is a put-together puzzle. She doesn't use *like* or *as*—one *is* the other.

Rosanne: Exactly. Katherine has shown us how you can write about common, regular things in new and surprising ways. As we practice our writing, keep this strategy in mind. Does anyone have anything to add?

Jonah shared the results of his conference, and then it was time to wrap up. Rosanne asked the students to write a new entry for homework using one or more of the find-a-topic strategies we discussed in class.

Follow-up

When the students shared their observations, Rosanne noticed that most students didn't have trouble finding an idea, but their writing focused on only one of the senses—sight. She decided to do a lesson on using the senses in description during the next writer's workshop. Later, she would do lessons that spurred students to discover ideas beyond their immediate surroundings. We often alter our plans depending on students' needs; this flexibility allows us to provide them with meaningful learning experiences because we offer instruction just when they need it and so are most receptive to it.

Rosanne selected a picture book that would show students how to use more than one sense when describing. She chose *Letting Swift River Go* by Jane Yolen because the author includes sensory details from four of the five senses and also uses metaphors and similes, techniques we have discussed and want our students to use in their own writing.

Reading this book sparked a conversation about when to use which sense. Jane Yolen did not use the sense of smell in her description; however, the story certainly does not seem lacking. This is an important conversation to have with students, because we want them to use only those senses that are most appropriate to what they are describing. For example, if a student were describing an apple pie, the use of sound probably wouldn't be important, but smell and taste would be imperative.

After Rosanne read the book aloud and charted what the students noticed, they returned to their notebooks to rewrite an entry or compose a new one incorporating the ideas and strategies noticed during the read-aloud. The chart appears below.

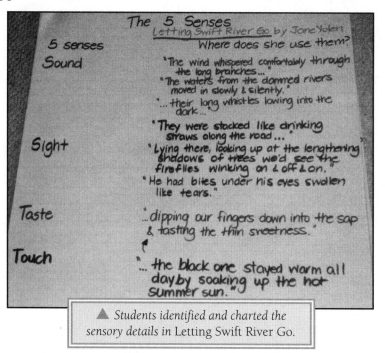

▲ *Students identified and charted the sensory details in* Letting Swift River Go.

Working With Similes and Metaphors

On another day, we return to *Letting Swift River Go* and discuss Yolen's use of similes and metaphors and how they conjure images. This technique is central to the book, and it builds on our previous discussion of metaphors and similes, in relation to Katherine's notebook entry. This is a good example of how we build students' knowledge by layering day after day, returning to writing elements that have already been discussed. Students in our classes explore this form of description in their writing; the following metaphors and similes are from student work:

"The sun is like a golden nugget, a fireball forever burning."

"Mist covers the river like the whiteness of a dove."

"The watermelon juice seeps through your teeth as water does through rocks on a windy beach day."

"Sophie smiled, her teeth shining like pearls."

"His hair is like rivers waiting to be set free."

"A banana is as yellow as the sun that awakens the day."

"The sky is so black the stars look like glowing jewels."

"The city's lights flicker like fireflies, off-on-off-on."

"The book has pulled me in like the sticky petals of a Venus fly trap and won't let me, the innocent fly, out."

"Seals stick out their little round heads like small sparkling silver balls glimmering in the sunlight."

"The spray of the sea stings my face like a million bumblebees."

"I kept one piece of chocolate in my mouth and it melted on my tongue, sliding down my throat like lava slowly dripping down the side of a volcanic rock surface."

Word Choice

Lesson by lesson, we take our cues from students about what strategy to teach next. We find that as students tackle new writing concepts, they often stumble over finding just the right words to express themselves. Therefore, early in the year we often focus on the word choices authors make. Choosing words that are "just right" is crucial in creating memorable imagery; spotlighting word choice at the beginning of the term focuses students on specific word use, important to many techniques we explore throughout the year.

Sample Lesson on Word Choice

To explore the importance of using "just the right word," Maria and her class studied how Crescent Dragonwagon's word choice affects the quality of writing in *Home Place*. This is an excerpt of their discussion.

✓ Discussion

Maria: What other words or phrases do you think were powerful in the book?

Raquel: He used some words differently. Like in the beginning when he said *trumpet*, he didn't mean it like an actual trumpet; he was giving a picture of what daffodils actually look like.

Maria: "Still they come up, these daffodils, cups lifted to trumpet the good news of spring. . . ." Oh, that's interesting; he also uses it as a verb.

Raquel: He also uses that word again when he says, "[They] trumpet their good news forever and forever."

Gabriel: Sometimes he uses two words to describe something and it somehow makes sense, like *scratchy-sweet* to describe a man's voice, and *quiet green* to describe the place.

Maria wraps up this discussion by asking, "So what makes for powerful word choices?" and guiding students to generate a list of criteria, as illustrated below.

Powerful Word Choice

* fresh, unusual images that surprise the reader: "yellow splash brighter than sunlight"

* vivid images that come alive for the reader: "honeysuckle-vined chimney"

* two words that don't usually go together but express the feeling you want to convey: "a man's voice, *scratchy-sweet*"

* words used in different ways—using a noun as a verb or adjective, for example: "trumpet the good news"

* specific, concrete nouns: *black walnut tree*

* vivid verbs that capture the action you want to describe: *rustle, nibble*

✓ Try It Out

After the discussion, Maria asked students to go back to their own writing and underline words they thought were too ordinary, such as *good* and *nice*. That night for homework they were to think of words that formed a clearer image and use them instead. The following day, before the next lesson, some of the students shared their revisions with the rest of the class. We created a chart with the old, tired words on one side and the new, improved words on the other; students copied this chart into their literature notebooks. This chart is displayed in the classroom, and when students come up with additional words, we add them to the chart.

> ▲ *Maria's class brainstormed alternatives to "tired" words.*

Follow-up Lesson

Most of the words discovered in Maria's class the previous day were adjectives, words that described nouns. Maria decided to extend the lesson by using William Steig's books, most of which have strong verbs.

✓ Introduction

Maria: I noticed that most of the words we talked about yesterday were adjectives, words that described nouns. I'd like us to think a little bit today about verbs, and how our choice of verbs affects our writing. William Steig is one of our favorite authors, and I'd like us to think about his verb choices for a while.

✓ Focus for Listening

Maria: I'm going to read *Amos & Boris*, and I'd like you to jot down any verbs you notice that stand out, that you think are particularly strong.

Maria reads story aloud.

✓ Discussion

Maria: Take a minute to look over your list, and compare it with a partner's.

Maria allows about three minutes for this activity.

Maria: Okay. What did you notice about Steig's word choice?

Alice: On the very first page he used *loved* three times. I think that set up a nice rhythm.

Sarah: I wrote down *bursting* from the first page—that's so strong and energetic. Definitely goes with the waves. I can almost hear them crashing.

Delia: I think those words help describe the setting really well, and they tell you about Amos, too.

Maria: That's a lot of work for a few verbs. What else did you notice?

Alice: I liked *marveled*; he used that when he was describing how Amos felt about being out at sea. It tells you just what Amos was feeling.

Havier: When he screamed when he fell off the boat, Steig used *squeaked*, which is good since Amos is a mouse. He couldn't really roar or have a strong voice. The verbs seemed to get a lot more active after that.

Josh: Yeah, *grabbed, evaded, bowling along* are all used after he fell off and is in the ocean.

Sarah: The next one I have is *burst* again, this time for Boris's head coming to the surface. I think of whales as graceful, but I guess it would seem like bursting to Amos, trying to stay afloat in the ocean.

Delia: And then Boris *loomed* over Amos. *Loomed* seems like a scary word to me, so I bet Amos was scared.

Maria: So you're saying that Steig's verb choice helps you get at what the characters are feeling.

Havier: It does, but the good verbs also seem to be where there is lots of action. Like when Boris dumped Amos off his back, Steig used *spluttering*, *splashing*, and *somersaulting*. Those are great, and help you see what Amos is doing.

The discussion continued until all students had shared and discussed the verbs on their lists.

✓ Try It Out

Maria asked students to work with a partner and read closely one of William Steig's books from the class library. Students created their own lists of Steig's verbs, and then the class came together to create a master listing of words they felt were strong. The chart, shown below, was hung in the classroom so students could borrow words during writing workshop.

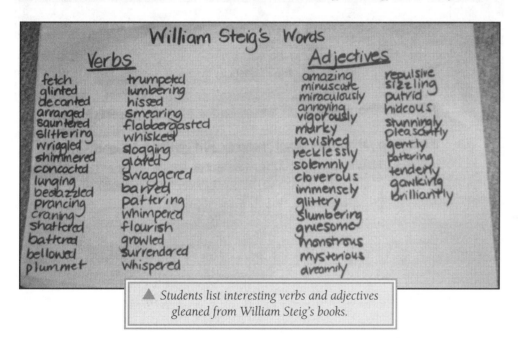

Verbs: fetch, glinted, decanted, arranged, sauntered, glittering, wriggled, shimmered, concocted, lunging, bedazzled, prancing, craning, shattered, battered, bellowed, plummet, trumpeted, lumbering, hissed, smearing, flabbergasted, whisked, slogging, glared, swaggered, barred, pattering, whimpered, flourish, growled, surrendered, whispered

Adjectives: amazing, minuscule, miraculously, annoying, vigorously, murky, ravished, recklessly, solemnly, cloverous, immensely, glittery, slumbering, gruesome, monstrous, mysterious, dreamily, repulsive, sizzling, putrid, hideous, stunningly, pleasantly, gently, pattering, tenderly, gawking, brilliantly

▲ *Students list interesting verbs and adjectives gleaned from William Steig's books.*

Recommended READING

William Steig is a master at creating interesting characters and engaging stories— and at choosing just the right words for his descriptions. We highly recommend any of his books for your study of word choice. Our favorites include:

Amos & Boris

Gorky Rises

Brave Irene

Shrek!

Doctor DeSoto

Two other great authors to study are Chris Van Allsburg and Patricia Polacco.

Through immersion, discussion, and practice, our students become excited about writing and look forward to a year filled with exploration and growth. These three to four weeks are crucial for setting the stage in our classrooms. We try to get our students comfortable with looking at picture books closely and turning to them for support in their writing. Many of the authors students encounter in these first few weeks become mentors for them. Students turn to these mentors often when looking for ways to get started or structure their piece, during revision, and for polishing their work. As the weeks progress, the students begin to develop a real sense of the qualities of good writing and to understand that they can incorporate those qualities into their own writing.

CHAPTER 3

▲ *A student turns to a picture book for inspiration.*

Planning and Writing Memoir

After we've done some of the introductory lessons described in the previous chapter, we begin our first writing cycle, during which students take an idea, develop it into a first draft, and then work it into a final version for publication. Since it's early in the year, we want to get to know our students better, and we want our students to get to know themselves as writers. Therefore, we often choose memoir for the first writing cycle because this genre encourages students to reflect on their lives and write about their own experiences. We want them to see that their lives are filled with stories and to learn the value of reflecting on those stories. Preteens and teens are often struggling with their identity, searching for their own sense of self, so this type of writing engages them on their favorite subject—themselves—and helps them work out some of their concerns.

The cycle takes three or four weeks to complete. It begins with students investigating picture books to discover what makes a memoir, continues with students choosing a particular topic from their own life and writing extensively about that topic, and culminates with a written draft, which is then revised, edited, and published. This chapter describes the planning and prewriting phase of a memoir-writing cycle; once this work is complete, students will be ready to draft their memoirs.

Mini-Inquiry: What Is a Memoir?

We begin the memoir-writing cycle by exploring students' prior knowledge of the genre. The following lesson from Maria's class introduces the memoir mini-inquiry. Maria gathers her students in the class meeting area and tells them that they are starting their first writing cycle on memoir.

Maria: Today we're going to explore a new kind of literature, called *memoir*. [Writes word on chart paper.] I'd like you to talk to a partner for a few minutes about you think this genre is.

Maria walks among the pairs of students as they discuss their ideas about memoir. Since they seem to have a basic understanding of the genre, she decides to move directly to the exploration phase. If your students do not have a basic understanding, you may want to begin with a discussion that provides enough background knowledge for students to begin an exploration.

Maria: Okay, you all seem to have some ideas about what a memoir is. We're going to explore this genre by reading and collecting books from our library that we think might be memoirs. You and a partner will be reading through our picture books and deciding whether you think they may or may not be memoirs. Remember to support your opinions about the books to convince your partner. If you both decide that a book might be a memoir, put it in the basket I have labeled POSSIBLE MEMOIRS, which will be in the middle of the meeting area. The books in the basket are possible memoirs that we will look at more closely as a class to define the elements of memoir.

The purpose of the lesson is to let students explore their ideas of memoir; Maria's job is simply to eavesdrop on conversations to get a sense of students' ideas.

As students are scouring the bookshelves and sharing their thoughts with one another, Maria walks around the room with a notebook, jotting down

TIP BOX

If your students have never been exposed to memoirs, you may want to begin your study by asking them if anyone has ever heard the word *memoir*. If not, ask them if it sounds like any other word. Students will inevitably come up with *memory*. From there you can guide a discussion that provides the basics of what a memoir is—a reflection on a memory or memories, in which the narrator or main character is the author. Then you can proceed with the lesson described here, filling in students' knowledge along the way.

some of the students' comments. This is one of the conversations she over-hears.

Sandy: This book is definitely a memoir. [Holds up a book.]

Josh: Why do you say that?

Sandy: Because it sounds like the author might be the character.

Josh: So?

Sandy: Memoirs are books that have "I" in them.

Josh: Yeah, but a lot of books have "I" in them; are they all memoirs?

Sandy: Well, I think if the "I" is the author. Let's put it in the basket anyway and we'll see.

After about 30 minutes of researching, Maria asks students to come back and share some of their thoughts. During their discussion, Maria jots down what the students are sharing. Some of their ideas about memoirs are accurate, while others are not. The purpose behind this lesson is not to tell the students what a memoir is, but to find out what they think it might be. They're generating their "thinking" about what they think they already know. At right are the notes Maria took during the first day's lesson.

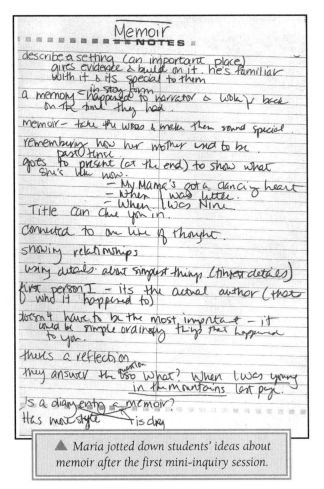

▲ *Maria jotted down students' ideas about memoir after the first mini-inquiry session.*

Follow-up

The next day Maria's students do the sorting activity for the first 15 minutes of class. Then students meet back on the rug, full of fresh ideas and questions about memoirs. Maria chooses a book out of the POSSIBLE

MEMOIRS basket and reads it aloud. This time it is *Fireflies* by Julie Brinckloe, and students listen intently, trying to decide if it's a memoir or not.

Maria: [Reads the book.] What do you think?

Manny: It's definitely not a memoir.

Maria: Why not?

Manny: Well, the book is written by a girl and the book's character is a boy.

Maria: So what you're saying is that a memoir has to be about the author and that the author has to be the main character. What does everybody else think?

Delia: Well, that kind of makes sense. But I'm not sure I agree. The book feels like a memoir should. You know it's about someone's experience trying to catch fireflies. And it's one experience, not a bunch.

Maria: So you think a memoir is one experience that is shared? Does anyone else have anything to add?

Nicky: I think it's a memoir because you feel like it could have happened—you feel like it's a real kid's memory. Who knows, the author could have been the little kid and changed the character to a boy, or it could have happened to her son and she wrote about it like he was telling the story. I don't think it really matters. It could have happened to any one of us or to any kid; it just feels like a real story.

Maria: What makes it feel like a real story?

Sydney: Lots of things. Like at the end when he doesn't understand why the fireflies aren't as beautiful when they are caught in a jar, and how he's upset because he knows he has to set them free.

Maria: Yes, he's reflecting on whether or not he should keep them.

Sydney: Yeah, and most kids have had something like that happen, and it really hurts to have to make a decision like that.

Tonda: Yeah, and the whole place, you know the setting, feels like a kid in the country. The author includes a lot of small details, like all the other kids are out, and the mother calls him to come in when it gets too late, and his parents talk to him like real parents would, and he knows about the scissors getting duller but does it anyway, like a regular kid.

As the conversation continues, Maria jots down on a chart what the class is discussing. She does not agree or disagree with what students are saying. Once again, she is only interested in listening to their comments and how they support their ideas with evidence from the book. The only aspect of memoir that the class seems to agree on is that all memoirs are about memories.

A useful way of having students compare two books they think might be memoirs is using a Venn diagram, as shown below for *Fireflies* and *When I Was Nine*. This technique allows students to see elements the books share, as well as ways in which they are different. The finished chart can be used for reference and helps students refine their criteria for memoir.

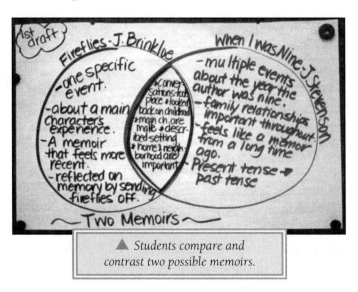

▲ *Students compare and contrast two possible memoirs.*

Our focus during the first week of our study is twofold: discussing what the students really know about memoir and immersing them in the genre. We read as many memoirs as possible—being sure to identify them as memoirs—to acquaint students with the ways memoirs sound, feel, and are written. Along the way, we refine our criteria for what makes a story a memoir, deriving from our study a standard definition. We sort out books we're not completely sure of, and we qualify some of the books we select, noting that because of the lack of memoirs written in picture book format, we often use fiction books that have the feel of a memoir as models for memoirs. We always supplement our reading of picture-book memoirs with excerpts taken from memoir collections, such as *Childtimes* by Eloise Greenfield and *The House on Mango Street* by Sandra Cisneros.

While some adults have a hard time seeing why a 12-year-old would write a memoir, we are careful to point out that memoirs are "the exploration of a memory, sometimes many memories" (Finn, 1999), and upper graders have just as much need to make meaning from their lives by reflecting on their memories as adults do. Some memoirs are about life-changing events, such as the death of your first dog or the moment you win your first trophy. But they can also be about ordinary times—first grade—or events—swimming class—that for the writer are special and unforgettable. For instance, in *My Mama Had a Dancing Heart*, Libba Moore Gray writes about her memories of her mother dancing. In all memoirs, writers examine their lives, and try to make sense of their experiences.

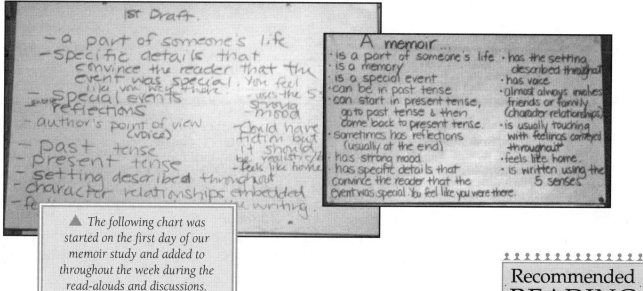

▲ *The following chart was started on the first day of our memoir study and added to throughout the week during the read-alouds and discussions.*

During the first week, students aren't writing as much as they have been in class because we are mostly talking about memoirs and reading them aloud, trying to work out their characteristics. However, homework assignments are geared toward writing about memories in our writer's notebooks, so students will have a lot of material to work with once they are ready to choose an idea and begin drafting.

To help our students generate entries that may develop into memoirs, we encourage them to write in the vein of the memoirs we read in class, and we provide them with a list of prompts they can use as starting points.

✳ What are your first memories of home?

✳ Have you ever moved? What was that like?

✳ What was your favorite activity as a preschooler? First grader? Third grader?

✳ How did you make your first friend?

✳ How did you feel when your best friend moved away?

✳ Write about pets you've had over the years.

✳ What has been the most significant event in your life? Why?

✳ What are the small, everyday moments that you treasure for some reason?

Recommended READING

Below are some adult memoirs you may enjoy, to get yourself ready for a discussion of memoir. Kids love hearing brief excerpts from the memoirs you're reading.

Memoirs of a Catholic Girlhood by Mary McCarthy

Angela's Ashes by Frank McCourt

This Boy's Life by Tobias Wolf

Little by Little by Jean Little

An American Childhood by Annie Dilliard

* Write about a trip you've taken that has had a lasting impact on you. It could be a cross-country vacation or a trip to the mall.

* Write about a special ritual or tradition your family celebrates.

* Interview family and friends about your past.

* Get out your old photos and free-write about them.

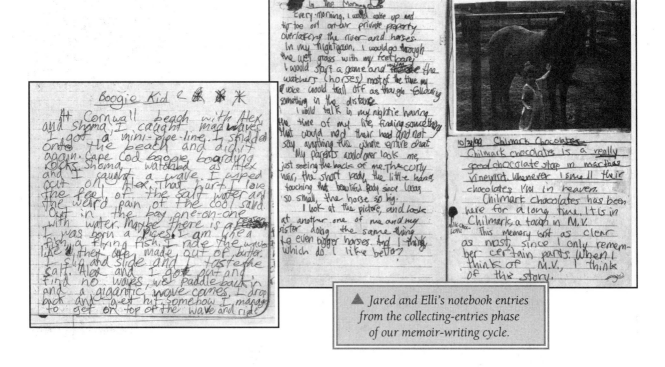

▲ *Jared and Elli's notebook entries from the collecting-entries phase of our memoir-writing cycle.*

Choosing a Seed From Your Notebook

It is the second week of our memoir study. We have already spent time reading memoirs, discussing memoirs, and choosing books we feel are in this genre. Through our read-alouds we have addressed many of the questions and uncertainties students had about various characteristics of memoir and have added to our chart. Students are regularly writing entries that feel like memoirs in their writer's notebooks.

After writing for about a week, Maria gathers her class in a circle in the meeting area.

Maria: I've been reading entries in your writer's notebooks, and I'm excited about what I've read. Today is the day we'll choose a seed idea from our writer's notebooks, the idea that we'll develop into a full-blown memoir.

First, I feel it might be best to do a little reading, you know, to whet our appetites. Find a quiet spot, either with a friend or alone, and read one of the picture book memoirs from our memoir baskets. In 20 minutes, I'm going to ask you to come back with your writer's notebooks, a pen or pencil, and one sticky-note.

During this time, Maria usually lingers in the meeting area with a few students who seem to need some extra support. Such decisions are based on what she's learned from their writer's notebooks and what she's noticed in class discussions.

After 20 minutes she asks everyone to come back to the meeting area.

Maria: Okay everybody, now that we're all in the memoir mood, let's think about how we can write our own. Here on my lap is my writer's notebook. I'm going to show you how I choose seed ideas. Listen to all of my thinking and watch what I'm doing, because this is how you will choose a seed from your writer's notebook.

Maria opens her notebook and flips through the pages. As she reads, she talks to herself aloud about all the questions and thoughts that are guiding her decisions.

Maria: Here's the entry about when I went to Greece for the first time. Wow, I loved this trip. I've got a lot to say about it, so maybe this will be my seed idea [puts the sticky-note there but continues to read on]. Oh, I really like this entry. I love the way I described my niece's laugh, but I don't think I have that much more to say. Even though I like the memory, I'll get stumped and frustrated when trying to add to it when drafting. [Continues scanning entries, but keeps her sticky-note on the Greece entry. Stops several pages later.] Wait, this is definitely the one. When I think about my childhood, half of my memories are set in our house in the country. Bike riding with my brothers, selling lemonade, tasting the honey from the honeysuckle bushes, learning how to swim in the bay. I've got so much more to say, and I feel so connected to this topic. Without having these memories of the house and everything we did there, I know I would not have had such a special childhood. This is definitely my seed idea.

Maria moves her sticky-note over and continues to look through her notebook but is set on her country house seed idea. She then addresses the class: "Okay, what did you notice me doing as I looked through my notebook?" The class describes Maria's thinking process and Maria records their responses. The chart on the next page is a list of what the class came up with.

Maria: Today, now, right here on the rug, you're going to reread your notebooks, moving the sticky notes around until you find the right seed. It should

TIP BOX

Doing the modeling activity on the overhead is very effective. That way, students can see the entries you're reading through and understand your think-aloud more easily.

49

be something meaningful to you, that you have a lot to say about, and that reveals part of you. Remember what I was saying out loud for you to hear? Well, that is what I'd like you to be doing in your mind. Make sure, though, that you keep it in your head so that those around you are not disturbed.

Students spend 10 to 15 minutes on this task. For homework, Maria asks them to take the seed idea and, without rereading their entry, write another entry about their chosen idea. For example, since Maria chose her country house as her seed idea, she would write that topic on a new page and start another entry, all without rereading what she had written before. We call this nurturing, or collecting around your seed—a term we borrow from Lucy Calkins—and use it to help students generate as many ideas as possible about their chosen topic.

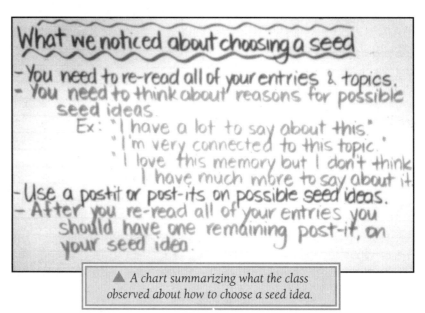

What we noticed about choosing a seed
- You need to re-read all of your entries & topics.
- You need to think about reasons for possible seed ideas.
    Ex: "I have a lot to say about this."
        "I'm very connected to this topic."
        "I love this memory but I don't think
            I have much more to say about it."
- Use a postit or post-its on possible seed ideas.
- After you re-read all of your entries you
    should have one remaining post-it, on
    your seed idea.

▲ *A chart summarizing what the class observed about how to choose a seed idea.*

Finding a Focus

After this one lesson on choosing a seed idea, a handful of students pre-dictably choose a seed idea that is too broad or overwhelming. To address this, Maria brought in pictures from her backpacking trip across Europe. She gathers a group of about six students who have bitten off a big topic and starts describing her trip, being sure to include lots of extraneous, humdrum details. It goes something like this:

This is when I went to Hungary. We were backpacking through Europe and this was the tenth country we visited. We started our trip in the first week of June, after graduating from college. We visited 13 countries and the whole trip was so much fun. I brought so much clothing with me. I remember I brought my red hat, three pairs of jeans, four T-shirts, five sweaters, some shorts, a bathing suit . . .

She continues to show the rest of her pictures and narrates every event that occurred. At this point, she is losing the students' attention and everyone is bored to pieces, including Maria.

When she feels she has gotten her point across, Maria throws the pictures on the floor and chooses only one picture to discuss. It happens to be the one where she is being escorted off a train by two police officers. She continues, "This is a part of the trip I will never forget. We were so scared. Just look at our faces. Our eyes were holding back buckets of tears, our shirts catching the sweat that was trickling down our backs." At this point she has redeemed herself. The students are perked up and she has everyone's attention. She knows that focusing on that one picture has helped to create a more meaningful and interesting story. She wants her students to realize this as well.

The group discusses which part of Maria's vacation they found most interesting. As you would expect, students all agree that the most interesting part was when she described the one picture, offering many exciting details. She gently reminds her students to focus their own memoirs on a meaningful, interesting event.

Trying It Out

Maria then asked students to go back to their seed idea and write the topic of their entry on the first line of a clean page. From there, she asked them to list all the possible stories they could write about that topic. If they could break any of those topics down further, then they should do so. Maria modeled this process for the class, using her trip to Europe as the example. Notice how she broke the general topic "individual countries" down to Hungary and Poland, and then further broke down Hungary into three possible stories.

> *My Trip Backpacking Through Europe*
>   *-My feelings*
>   *-Individual countries*
>   *-Finding hostels*
>   *-Living with the same two people for two months*
>   <u>*Individual Countries*</u>
>   *-Hungary*
>   *-Poland*
>   <u>*Hungary*</u>
>   *-Our apartment*
>   *-Frosted flakes*
>   *-Almost getting arrested*

Maria explains, "It's like when you tell a friend about a movie. You talk about certain parts, the ones that were the most exciting, or the parts that moved you, made you laugh or cry. As a writer, you should think about times in your own life that stand out, maybe because they were exciting, or maybe because they were emotional. These are the parts you should write about in your entries, always narrowing the topic down to the most critical feeling, moment, or event." This activity helps students stay focused as they continue to gather entries around their seed idea, helping it to grow.

Drafting a Memoir

▲ *Two students work on their memoirs.*

Now that students have chosen their seed ideas and gathered lots of entries around them, they are ready to work on actually crafting their memoir pieces. We ask students to reread the entries written around their seed ideas and ask themselves, *What does this say about me? How can I share with my readers what this means to me?* We remind them of the choices they have as writers and ask them to consider thoughtfully how they will construct their piece.

Voice

We encourage students to think about what voice they want to use: Will they write as themselves as they currently are? Will they use the voice of an earlier self? We remind them to make sure their language and rhythm match the voice they've chosen and fit the events they're narrating. We also caution them to use a consistent voice throughout, so as not to confuse the reader.

Details

Students need to think about which details are important to include. How important is the setting? Are there other characters that need to be described? Does action play a big role in the memoir? Is there an important object readers need to visualize? What feeling do I want to evoke in my readers? Identifying the critical elements of memoir helps students focus their attention and use the strategies we've discussed to portray them vividly.

Structure

Students need to consider how they will connect the events in their memoirs. Do they want to retell events chronologically? Do they want to incorporate flashbacks? How many? Will one carefully placed flashback work? Will they use a recurring line to provide structure? Revisit an image or sound or event from the beginning at the end? We ask students to think about the story they want to tell and choose a structure that fits.

Choosing a Mentor Book

Moving from an entry in their writer's notebooks to a fully developed narrative piece is quite a leap, and students need a lot of support to negotiate that leap successfully. While the questions above provide a starting point, we have found that encouraging students to use a particular picture book as a mentor, or model, supports them during their writing. Some students choose one book while others may choose a few books by one author, and still others might use one book for its structure and another for its mood.

Rosanne returned to the books she had read during the mini-inquiry in her class and asked her students to think specifically about the structure of the stories— how they began, what sorts of details were included, how scenes were connected, and how the stories ended. She referred to the charts from the previous week that addressed the language used, the rhythm of the writing, and the special

▲ *Students search for a model memoir.*

We both have at least 30 to 40 memoirs (with multiple copies included) so students can take the books home and refer to them while working there. If you don't yet have quite this many, consider checking some out of your local or school library, or ask students to bring in memoirs they have from home to share with the class. You can also borrow from colleagues, perhaps even starting a collection for your school to share.

words the class noticed in the memoirs. These were the elements she wanted students to think about and weave into their pieces. For the remaining 30 minutes of writing workshop, Rosanne asked students to reread the memoirs in the picture book baskets, noticing what elements they might like to try out in their own writing. Students then chose one or more books that sounded and looked the way they envisioned their memoir; these books became their guides throughout the drafting and revising process. Their homework each night was to read the books and think about how they could incorporate various elements they found into their own memoirs. They were not required to use specific strategies from books, but rather to study how one (or more) authors handled similar issues in their work.

Lesson Extension

To help students generate plenty of details for their memoirs, try some of the following activities:

* Have students choose one line from their memoir that they have lots more to say about, put it on the top of a new page, and write everything they can about it.

* Remind them to describe scenes or experiences using sensory details (see Chapter 2).

* Focus their attention on beginnings and endings (see Chapter 6).

After two weeks of defining memoir, writing about memories, choosing a seed idea, and then writing all about that idea, students are ready to come out of their notebooks and draft their memoirs with the help of picture book mentors. The next chapter focuses on mood, voice, and point of view, elements that enrich any piece of writing and that proved challenging to our students as they drafted their first memoirs of the year.

▲ *Students work together, exploring how writers create mood.*

CHAPTER 4

Exploring Mood, Voice, and Point of View

S tories that touch our hearts and remain etched in our minds usually have a rich mood, clear voice, and are told from a distinct perspective. These three writing elements infuse a piece with its personality, attitudes, and feelings. The mood is entwined with the voice telling the story. Since these three elements—mood, voice, and point of view—are so connected and so enmeshed in creating memorable writing, we teach and study them together.

While these elements are closely related, they have subtle differences that we must draw out for our students. *Mood* is the atmosphere of a piece, the feel of it, and the emotions it evokes in you. *Voice* is the personality in the piece—the way you can hear a ten-year-old child's or an old woman's personality coming through in the narration. It breathes life into a story, article, or report and helps establish the mood. *Point of view* is the perspective from which the author chooses to convey his or her idea; it can be first or third person, limited or omniscient.

Making students aware of voice and point of view helps them create the mood they want in their own writing. Knowing that they can write from one of several perspectives, and use a particular voice (not necessarily their own), gives them choices and ideas for how to craft a story to create a particular mood. The lessons in this chapter demonstrate how we use picture books to introduce these three elements to our students and help them transfer these techniques to their own writing.

Focus on Mood

In October our students were writing the first draft of their memoirs, as described in the previous chapter. While the stories were about interesting and important aspects of our students' lives, few succeeded in engaging the reader. The student writers couldn't seem to find their voices or re-create the feelings the episode evokes for them. Since the stories were missing a sense of mood and a distinct voice, we decided to focus our next few lessons on these elements.

Our first step was to choose a picture book with a strong mood, so students could easily identify it and see the writing techniques used to create it. We've found that Charlotte Zolotow's *The Storm Book* works; in just the first three pages, she shifts the mood three times.

Sample Lesson on Mood

We provide students with copies of the first three pages of *The Storm Book* and either read them aloud or have students read them to themselves. Our discussion goes something like this:

✓ **Focus for Listening**

Rosanne: We are going to be reading a few pages from *The Storm Book* by Charlotte Zolotow. I want you to silently read the three pages I give you all the way through. While you read, I want you to be conscious of what you're feeling. These copies are yours, so you can write on them. You should underline the parts that make you feel a particular way. [Alternatively, you can read the text aloud; students would take notes while you read.]

Rosanne hands out the text. When everyone finishes reading, she begins a discussion.

Book Excerpt:

The Storm Book

It is a day in the country, and everything is hot. The grass looks dry and parched. The buttercups are sticky with dust; the daisies' white petals look gray; and all the flowers, the rambler roses climbing up the gate, the hollyhocks leaning against the house, hang limply on their stems.

The little boy can almost see the heat quivering up like mist from the earth. A little caterpillar climbs carefully up a dusty blade of grass and then climbs down again. There is a special hot stillness over everything. The white fox terrier has crawled under the latticework of the porch and lies sleeping in the shade. Even the birds seem too hot to sing, for there is not a sound among the leaves.

But the hazy sky begins to shift, and the yellow heat turns gray. Everything is the same color—one enormous listless gray world where not a breath stirs and the birds don't sing. There isn't the slightest motion of a branch, the slightest whisper of a breeze. And still there is something expectant in the growing darkness; something is astir, something soundless and still for which the little boy waits.

He waits and he sees dark clouds beginning to form, throwing their shadow over the parched fields, moving one after another until they cover the sky and the world is black as night. A little cool wind suddenly races through the trees, sways the rambler roses, bends the daisies and buttercups and Queen Anne's lace and the long grass until they make a great silver sighing stretch down the hill.

Then it happens! Shooting through the sky like a streak of starlight comes a flash so beautiful, so fast, that the little boy barely has time to see the flowers straining into the storm wind.

"Oh, Mother," he calls, "what was that?"

Recommended READING

Voice and Point of View:

Chicken Sunday by Patricia Polacco

Gila Monsters Meet You at the Airport by Marjorie Sharmat

Knots on a Counting Rope by Bill Martin Jr.

My House Has Stars by Megan McDonald

My Momma's Kitchen by Jerdine Nelen

The Pain and the Great One by Judy Blume

The River Ran Wild by Lynne Cherry

The Kapok Tree by Lynne Cherry

The True Story of the Three Little Pigs by Jon Scieszka

Through Grandpa's Eyes by Patricia MacLachlan

When I Was Young in the Mountains by Cynthia Rylant

"Alexander" books by Judith Viorst

✓ **Discussion**

Rosanne: So what did you feel?

Sarah: It's all dull; on the first page everything is supposed to be so still. It seems slow and lazy, like you feel on a hot summer day.

Henry: Yeah, she spends a lot of time on small details, too. I mean, who notices a caterpillar climbing up a blade of grass? I wouldn't notice it. It gives you a whole idea of the surroundings and makes you feel slow and lazy—there's so much time, you watch a caterpillar in the grass.

TIP BOX

In our classes, students say "ditto" when they agree with what another person has said. This allows the conversation to flow without being repetitive.

Rosanne: Okay. You felt maybe dullness and slowness.

Jeremiah: On the second page it describes how the branches are still: "There isn't the slightest motion of a branch, the slightest whisper of a breeze."

Rosanne: So it's quiet.

Carol: Ditto and "something soundless."

Sarah: The first page starts out slowly. Then it builds and she just throws it all in at the end. Like it says here [points to text]: "Then it happens! Shooting through the sky like a streak of starlight comes a flash so beautiful, so fast, that the little boy barely has time to see the flowers straining into the storm wind."

Rosanne: Good.

Stephen: "Then it happens!" is exciting. And it's different from the first part—the sentence is so short.

Rosanne: So the change in sentence length signals a change in feeling, from dullness to excitement.

Carol: Yes, and before that on the second page [student reads], "But the hazy sky begins to shift, and the yellow turns gray." The fact that she used *shift* and *turns* tells us that something is changing and makes it sound like something is going to happen. Also here on the same page, "And still there is something expectant in the growing darkness; something is astir; something soundless and still for which the little boy waits."

Stephen: It's like she's building suspense.

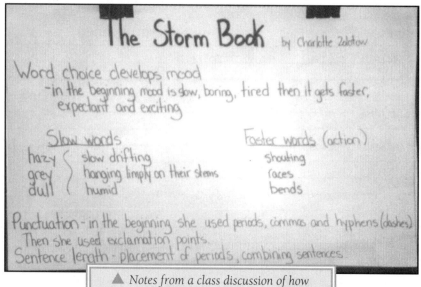

▲ *Notes from a class discussion of how mood is established in* The Storm Book.

Rosanne: What exactly in the sentences creates the suspense?

Sarah: Well, she talks about "something"—she uses it three times. And we don't know what that something is, so it makes us wonder.

Rosanne: So repetition of a word, especially a word that doesn't give away what's happening. Sometimes these are called *word referents*. Good. Anything else?

Mark: The words after *something* build suspense, too—make you feel like something's going to happen.

Rosanne: What words?

Mark: *Expectant*, first. Then *astir*—but you don't know what's moving. And the boy waits.

Rosanne: Good. Let's read the sentence again and see if we notice anything else that builds suspense. [Reads sentence aloud.]

Yasmeen: What about *soundless* and *still*?

Rosanne: How do they build suspense?

Yasmeen: Well, the boy is waiting for something, and something's moving, but yet it's *soundless* and *still*. It seems, like, ominous.

Rosanne: Excellent. So repetition, using vague or indefinite words, and creating a contrast with adjectives can help build suspense. Do you guys know what it is called when a feeling is created in literature? The events in a story are the *plot*; the place of the story is called the *setting* . . .

Kareem: Mood.

Rosanne: Yes, *mood*. Has anyone else heard of that?

Group nods yes.

Rosanne: Okay, now let's talk about how Charlotte Zolotow created the shifting moods. How do authors do that? You guys were touching upon it when you were supporting your feelings with examples from the text. We've already mentioned three different feelings. Who'd like to recap?

Jeremiah: At first everything is dull and lazy and not going very fast. She writes, "A gray world"; everyone thinks of gray as a dull color.

Kareem: Then there's the feeling of suspense: "The little boy waits," and on the next page, "He waits and sees." You want to know what he's waiting for.

Carol: And here, "Shooting through the sky like a streak of starlight."

There's action there, and excitement.

Rosanne: Okay. You've mentioned three different moods—the feelings of stillness, suspense, and excitement. And we've talked about how she created those moods. Now let's look at how she changed the mood.

Kareem: She put in some action.

Rosanne: How does she show the action? Let's look at that.

Stephen: She uses that really short sentence with the exclamation point—that shows a big change. Before that, the sentences are long and spend a lot of time describing little things, like the caterpillar. After that, the whole feel changes—there's more energy: "streak of starlight," a "flash so beautiful, so fast," and "flowers straining."

Rosanne: Okay, you've pointed to sentence length and punctuation as an indicator of change, and talked about the differences before and after that one sentence.

Sarah: Yes, and she's also so descriptive.

Rosanne: In what part?

Sarah: Especially in the beginning, where she just described every little thing, like when it's so hot and sticky. She uses all these details.

Jeremiah: Yeah, and in the end it just changes your whole view of the piece. She's still using details, but so much happens in just one sentence. If you didn't read that one line, this whole piece would seem so dull, but after this one short paragraph, the whole sense or mood of the piece changes.

Rosanne: Do you think the kind of details a writer chooses can affect mood?

Sarah: Yeah, but it's also the words you use.

Rosanne: Yes, word choice is important. Let's look at that.

Tanya: It's like when she writes, "But the hazy sky begins to shift, and the yellow heat turns gray." If you changed *gray* to *red* you'd get an entirely different mood.

The discussion continued, and the students noticed that word choice is critical in creating mood. The students also noticed the rhythm of the writing. In the beginning the sentences seem to meander, and in the end they are shorter. To tie up the discussion, Rosanne asked students to categorize the strategies they observed for setting and changing mood; the result is shown in the chart on the next page.

Ways to Set a Slow Mood
- Write long, slow-paced sentences
- Use longer words
- Use calm, quiet words
- Be very descriptive
- Make it seem like time is moving slowly

Ways to Build Suspense
- Use short sentences
- Use strong action verbs
- Use words that are exciting
- Leave hints for the reader
- Use indefinite nouns and pronouns
- Choose details that convey action

Ways to Change the Mood
- Change sentence structure
- Use different kinds of words

✓ Try It Out

By the end of the discussion, students have some ideas for creating mood in their own work. Rosanne invites them to try it out on their own. Students write in their writer's notebooks an entry on any topic with a specific mood in mind. We encourage them to create the mood using the strategies we discuss in class. Some moods our students have tried to describe include *angry*, *sad*, *playful*, *still*, *exciting*, and *embarrassing*.

> Isabella:
> As she stood, sandy and cold, on the beach, the fireflies swarmed in clumps. the shells around her made delicate patterns laid by the hand of the ocean, the slow motion of the waves created a rhythm to which her heart beat. Above her, a full moon rose, casting a gentle, shimmering glow on the sand. Then it happened. Shooting through the sky in a graceful arc, the star sailed straight and strong, as though shot from an arrow. The beauty of it all.

▲ *Isabella works on a quiet, peaceful mood.*

After students have tried to craft an entry that gets across a particular mood, we have a class share. While conferring with students, we choose one or two who seem to have gotten the hang of it and ask them to share. We ask the student to read his or her piece while we listen and try to figure out what mood the author was going for. This is when the class gives feedback and suggestions on what the student has done well and ideas for improving his or her piece. We also try to name the specific strategies the student used. We continually refer to the chart we created during the lesson. We always remind students to turn to the authors of the books they're reading independently as well to see how they create powerful moods.

Additional Book Selections for Mood

In *My Mama Had a Dancing Heart*, Libba Moore Gray does several things to create a light and playful mood. First, she creates an energy and sense of fun by making up hyphenated, alliterative words that make you want to get up and move: *tip-tapping, song-singing, finger-snapping*. She also alternates short and long sentences, with the short sentences literally commanding the reader to act—to *bless the world* and to *celebrate*. It all results in a delightful mood that captures the mother's effervescent attitude toward life and engages the reader with her enthusiasm.

> Bless the world
> it feels like
> a tip-tapping
> song-singing
> finger-snapping
> kind of day.
> Let's celebrate.
>
> —from *My Mama Had a Dancing Heart* by Libba Moore Gray

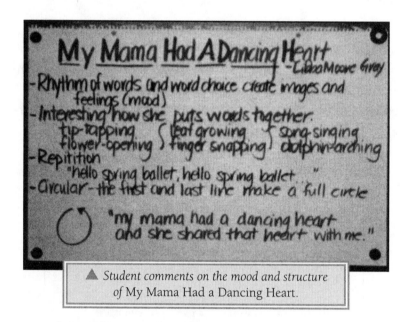

▲ *Student comments on the mood and structure of* My Mama Had a Dancing Heart.

Another book we use for mood is *Daydreamers* by Eloise Greenfield. This book is particularly good for showing how rhythm can create a mood, and for demonstrating how grammatical constructions can contribute to and signal a change in mood. When Greenfield is talking about the dreamers themselves, she uses the present participle form of verbs—*holding, letting, thinking, looking*—which gives the sense that the dreamer is acting and in control. Then she signals a change with the word *while*, a subordinating conjunction. Now the subjects shift from daydreamers to their dreams and thoughts, and the actions are expressed with a different verb form, the present tense. These verbs are playful and follow a delightful pattern: two compound words (usually the names of games) are followed by a single-syllable word—*hopscotch, doubledutch, dance; rollerskate, crisscross, bump.* The mood in this section is jaunty and full of energy, and it ends with the end of the sentence.

Things slow down again in the ninth line; we are back to the dreamers with their actions expressed in present participles—*thinking, looking, planning.* The change in verb form highlights the contrast between the dreamers and the dreams; using the subordinating conjunction *while* to introduce the dreams suggests that the dreams, while lively and soaring, are in the service of the dreamers. In the last few lines the dreamers use their wild thoughts for *thinking, planning, asking,* moving them from the dream world to the rational world. Finally, their hands move again, bringing them back to reality and putting their dreams into action.

> Daydreamers . . .
>
> holding their bodies still
> for a time
> letting the world turn around them
>
> while their dreams hopscotch,
> doubledutch, dance,
>
> thoughts rollerskate,
> crisscross,
> bump into hopes and wishes.
>
> Dreamers thinking up new ways,
> looking toward new days,
>
> planning new tries,
> asking new whys.
> Before long,
> hands will start to move again.
>
> —from *Daydreamers*
> by Eloise Greenfield

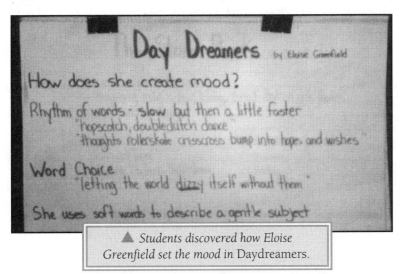

▲ *Students discovered how Eloise Greenfield set the mood in* Daydreamers.

We read these books, as well as many others, discussing the various techniques authors use to create mood. Do not feel you have to dig out every nuance in a story, but encourage students to read deeply and critically.

Voice and Point of View

After we've introduced mood, we discuss voice and point of view, talking about how they can contribute to mood. We try changing the voice and point of view of a piece and notice the effect that has on the story. A few of the lessons we teach to help students understand and use voice and point of view follow.

Voice

A book we like to use to launch our discussion of voice is *Tight Times* by Barbara Shook Hazen. It's a poignant story about a young boy whose parents won't let him get a dog because of financial hardship. In large part, the poignancy is due to the boy's voice that comes through so vividly in the story. He cannot understand why he can't have a dog. The explanation of "tight times" is meaningless to him, so he takes matters into his own hands by adopting a cat.

Book Excerpt: *Tight Times*

I tiptoed into the kitchen. I tried to be quiet. But the milk was up too high. It tipped and made a terrible mess. Mommy and Daddy ran out of their rooms. Daddy looked funny. He looked at the cat. Then he looked at me. "What is that!" he asked. "It's a cat," I told him. "A nice lady said I could keep it. And I didn't go near the street." Then something sort of scary happened. Daddy started to cry. So did Mommy. I didn't know daddies cried. I didn't know what to do. Then they both made a sandwich hug with me in the middle. So I started to cry.

The boy's voice comes through in the short sentences he uses to narrate this incident and in the way he interprets the events. His parents are moved because the boy's desire for a pet was so strong that it led him to bend their rules, although we can tell he's usually conscientious about keeping them: he didn't go near the street; he tried not to disturb his parents; he's concerned about making a mess. He doesn't know what to make of their show of emotion, so he resorts to crying himself. The word choice, sentence length, and dialogue help the young boy's voice shine through.

Choosing an appropriate voice for a piece depends on the narrator—who is speaking—and the audience—who is being addressed. For memoirs, the speaker is the student; we help students bring their own voice to their pieces by suggesting they pretend they're speaking to a friend. For nonfiction—for example, an editorial—the voice is still the student's, but thinking of the intended audience becomes important when deciding how to express that voice. We often encourage students to talk into a tape recorder or to a partner the way they'd like to sound addressing their audience; then they can play it back and try to capture that voice in their writing. For fiction, when students usually adopt the voice of a character, their knowledge of the character helps them choose which of the strategies we've discussed will best bring out the strong and unique voice of that character.

Point of View

It's difficult, if not impossible, to separate voice and point of view, as evidenced by the above example. Our discussion of voice in *Tight Times* naturally leads us to point of view. One reason we like to use this book is that it provides the perspective of the father juxtaposed with that of the son. Take a look at this excerpt from the book, in which the father is trying to explain "tight times" to his son.

Book Excerpt: *Tight Times*

He said tight times are when everything keeps going up.
I had a balloon that did that once.
Daddy said tight times are why we all eat Mr. Bulk instead of
    cereals in little boxes.
I like little boxes better.
Daddy said tight times are why we went to the sprinkler last
    summer instead of the lake.
I like the lake better.
Daddy said tight times are why we don't have a roast beef on
    Sunday.
Instead we have soupy things with lima beans. I hate lima beans.
If I had a dog, I'd make him eat mine.

Each of the father's explanations is followed by the child's response. The gulf of understanding between the two is highlighted by this rhetorical structure, which serves as a wonderful jumping-off point for a discussion of point of view. We encourage students to be aware of the words they choose when writing and provide them with plenty of picture book models of effective use of voice and point of view.

Two Characters, Two Stories, One Plot

Another good book for exploring point of view is *The Pain and the Great One* by Judy Blume. The book is divided into two parts, "The Pain" and "The Great One." Each part is told from the point of view of one of the characters and thus has its own distinct voice. As you can imagine,

although the situation is the same, the stories are quite different, thus providing our students with another clear example of how voice and point of view can play a major role in shaping a piece of writing.

Point of view and voice are difficult concepts for young writers to apply to their own writing. To help them choose a perspective and voice for their stories and reports, we present them with the following guidelines.

❊ Think about the event, issue, or topic you're planning to write about. From whose point of view do you want to write? Whose point of view seems natural to you?

❊ Once you've decided on a point of view, remember to stick with it throughout your piece!

❊ Now think about the voice you want to use to convey your ideas.

Adopting Alternate Points of View

Two Bad Ants by Chris Van Allsburg is an ideal text for teaching and learning about point of view. This book is about two ants who stay behind in a bowl of "crystals" and all the adventures they encounter while stuck in a kitchen. When the ants get scooped out of the "crystals" (a bowl of sugar) and find themselves in a cup of coffee, their troubles have just begun. Our students easily see how someone's point of view or perspective can change the way he sees a situation and in turn reacts. What would seem like a harmless cup of coffee to humans is a bitter lake with treacherous waves to the ants. Students begin to realize that there are many ways a story can be told, and they look forward to experimenting with that idea.

Jon Scieszka writes popular children's stories from different points of view. One book is *The True Story of the Three Little Pigs*, written from the wolf's perspective. Using Jon Scieszka as a model, we sometimes have students rewrite familiar stories, such as *Little Red Riding Hood* and *Cinderella*, from a new point of view or perspective. This activity helps them to internalize this element of writing.

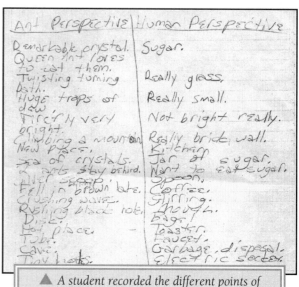

▲ *A student recorded the different points of view in* Two Bad Ants *in his literature notebook.*

✓ Conference

Since Casey had struggled with mood and point of view in her last piece, Rosanne wanted to talk with her about these elements so she would think about them before beginning her draft. Below is a transcript of the conference; Casey's final piece, "30-53rd," is on page 69.

Rosanne: What is this piece going to be about?

Casey: I noticed that I had written a lot of entries about when I was little and going to the playground, so I thought I would write about that.

Rosanne: Sounds good. Have you thought about what kind of mood you want the piece to have?

Casey: I want it to be fun and light. Like how a little kid sees things.

Rosanne: So you want a playful mood and you want to write it from the perspective of a young child. Did I understand you correctly?

Casey: Yeah.

Rosanne: Okay, how do you think you will go about doing that?

Casey: I'm not sure yet. I think I may look at some of the picture books in the class to see if I can find any that are about a little kid playing.

Rosanne: That's a great idea, and, you know, you can also look for books that have the playful mood you are looking for. They don't necessarily have to be about a child playing. Once you find some model books, try to notice the rhythm of the words. And, of course, notice the word choice.

Casey: I can do that.

Rosanne: You may want to look at some Jane Yolen and Patricia Polacco books. I think they may help you.

Casey: Okay.

Rosanne: When you're writing, remember to include the little details that will make the story come alive. If you write about, say, a slide, be sure to include why it was so great for you as a kid. What did it look like? What did it feel like? How did you feel sliding down it? Maybe you can go to the playground this weekend and just watch the kids playing. That may help, too. All right, do you know what you're going to do?

Casey: Yes, first I'm going to look for some picture books.

Rosanne: What will you be looking for?

Casey: Well, I'm going to look for the words they use. First, I'm going to find books that have the mood that I want; then I'm going to notice the words they use and also the rhythm. How it sounds. And when I start writing, I'm going to try to be really specific and write about the little details.

Rosanne: That sounds like a plan. Don't forget, if you can, to go to the playground and watch the little kids.

Rosanne gave Casey some specific tips based on her goals for her piece. She made sure Casey had a plan in mind before ending the conference; follow-up conferences helped Casey develop the playful mood she was looking for.

Students at Work

It's critical that we constantly assess students' work to determine how effective our teaching has been. You can see how well students have internalized the idea of mood, voice, and point of view by looking at the progress Casey made over the course of about a month spent focusing on these three literary elements. Both pieces began as entries in her writer's notebook, and she chose to develop them into published pieces. From a flat first story written when our discussions about mood and voice were in their infancy, she moved on to create one with a playful mood. The result demonstrates the power of lessons and conferences focusing on mood, voice, and point of view.

September 30

Music

I play the flute.

I have been playing since January and my teacher, Suzanne, has taught me many easy pieces or notes and many hard ones. At the beginning, at my first music lesson, I had no clue how to play anything, and I got frustrated very easily. Most of the things that used to be hard are much simpler now, because of all the times I practiced and I remembered all of the tips Suzanne had given me. In fact, I have improved so much that she suggested that I play in Orchestra. I did, and loved it.

A trumpet, French horn, violins, cellos, flutes, we all play together in the same Orchestra. Just like my music lessons, I was horrible at first, but got better very quickly. One of the things that I have not quite yet mastered is keeping the same time, or beat, as everyone else I play with. I have noticed that many other kids, especially violins (they have the back beat), have come up with their own ways of counting time for themselves. Some of those ways are tapping your foot, and counting in your head.

Everyone has learned how to play many different pieces, some low, some high, some hard, some easy. The higher ones are not ear-piercing screechy sounding, but are still hard to keep clear. The lower notes are easier because you do not need to take such deep breaths and they sound good no matter what. A line from a book I read reminded me of the low notes, and the reason I remember it so well is probably because those are my favorite ones, " . . . as low and as deep as a bullfrog's voice . . ."

November 5

30–53rd

When I was about four years old, every weekday afternoon in the fall was spent playing in the park. We called it 30-53rd because it was at 35th Street and 3rd Avenue, which I translated into 30-53rd.

My baby-sitter, Lori, would bundle me up in warmish clothes, or she'd attempt to dress me in layers. As I remember, this process was not very much fun for me and now that I think back, it probably wasn't much fun for Lori either. I would twist and wriggle, bending my back so Lori had to struggle when putting my clothes on. The stroller was next. As soon as I was in the seat and buckled, I would try to get out. I don't know why, but it was probably because I did not get to do it all on my own. Some days, when Lori was in a good mood, she would let me try to buckle myself. After about four tries, she would take it away from me and buckle me in herself.

When we finally got downstairs, for the first couple of blocks, I just looked straight ahead of me, with sort of a dull stare. When we came fairly close to the park, I would start smiling. There were so many kids to play with now! And most of them were my age!

Katie, my good friend who lived nearby, was often there, too. We would usually run for "the big kid swings," as we called them. Those swings were the best kind: smooth, black, and they smelled strange, like rubber bands. They were a little too high off the ground for us four-year-olds, and when one of us first tried to climb up onto one, we would slip and land stomach down on the swing. Our legs would be sticking out behind us and our arms would be straight out in front of us. Katie found that letting one's legs drop to the ground, running forward while still holding onto the swing, then lifting your feet up as you went backward, made you feel like you were flying! To this day, I still do that.

The thing we both loved to do the most was next: the slide. It was a beautiful, long, silver and red metal slide. From the ground, the top seemed very far away. Once I got to the top, I would sit down on the cold metal, worn smooth from the many rides of many children. I would sit for a minute, looking around and enjoy being taller than everyone. Then, whoosh, I was off! Down, down, down the slide I went. The wind blowing my hair around my face like feathery stalks of wheat in a field in the middle of a storm. Down, down, down, the ride was never-ending. All of a sudden, everything stopped. The ride was over. I would do that about five times. Then I would run around with Katie and play tag, or hide-and-seek, always hiding in the same places: me under the slide, Katie behind a tree.

After ten minutes of this, Lori would come over and we would go through the whole stroller thing again. Only this time I would be crying most of the time. I wanted to go with Katie! I wanted to play more!

When we got home, Lori would undress me and put me to bed for my afternoon nap. At first I would protest, but sleep would find me and take me away, so that tomorrow and the day after and forever, I could go play in the park I named 30-53rd.

Voice and Point of View in Nonfiction

Following are examples where students successfully incorporated voice and point of view into their nonfiction writing.

Some people just need others to count on, isn't that right? An idol, a god, or to my little brother, me. To tell you the truth, he's actually my cousin. But our bond is something beyond cousins, for his one flight to America utterly changed my life.
—by Rich, fifth grader, from a memoir

The best way to describe the twenties is frantic and chaotic with all the new inventions and the stock market booming. The thirties was the home of the Great Depression: enough said right there. This time period needed leaders. No, not presidents: they needed heroes and mentors, someone to guide them through everything. Many people were suited to do the job, but few stood out to reach their nation. This book explains the lives of six of those people and how they made good mentors. The six people we chose to write about are Susan B. Anthony, Amelia Earhart, Louis Armstrong, Leroy Paige, Babe Ruth, and Mohandas Gandhi. Maybe if more people helped out, Americans would not have suffered during the thirties as they did.

—from a sixth-grade group social studies project

Have you ever tasted the school lunch at our school? Well, if you haven't there's only one way to describe it . . .. Maybe you are wondering how I know about the lunch. Well, for four and a half years, I had to survive school lunch. Until my parents saved me and agreed to make my lunch. However, my friend is forced to eat school lunch every day. He usually eats little or none, and from what he tells me, school breakfast is not any better. So it is time for some changes.

—by Thomas, fifth grader, from an editorial

If you like the C.S. Lewis series, you'll love this series. If you've read one of Lewis's books, you can imagine what *The Hobbit* is like. Both are mystical, with sorcery and evil enchantments. They talk about the same thing—freeing a kingdom from the mystical evils of the world. They are sophisticated, exciting, suspenseful, and amazing. Both are science fiction, and have settings that are totally different from our world. But maybe they are like life. You need motivation no matter what it may be . . .. The ring that Bilbo found gave him tons of possibilities. The ring represented his motivations, the thing that gave him courage. So what's your motivation?

—by Richard, fifth grader, from a book review

In this chapter, we introduced three different literary elements that enhance our students' writing and discussed specific strategies writers use to create mood, voice, and point of view. By reading picture books, students are able to articulate strategies and then transfer the knowledge into their own writing, as demonstrated in the lessons. We revisit these elements throughout the year in both fiction and nonfiction writing cycles.

As you can see from the student work in this chapter, focusing on mood, voice, and point of view pays big dividends in the quality of student writing. As they learn to play with word choice and rhythm, and to choose a voice and point of view that contribute to a particular mood, students are on their way to creating memorable stories. These lessons help in their first memoir pieces, and they also apply to the next genre we teach, realistic fiction, which we discuss in the next chapter.

CHAPTER 5

▲ *Maria leads a lesson on realistic fiction.*

Planning and Writing Realistic Fiction

Harry Potter, Amazing Grace, Gilly Hopkins, Maniac McGee—we are drawn to these characters because they are complex, credible, and sympathetic. We feel as though we know them, and we recognize something of ourselves in them. We know what they look like, how they dress, what they like and don't like, how their voices sound, what their fears and dreams are. Vividly drawn, they live on in our imaginations long after we finish reading their stories.

Novelists and short story writers realize the importance of creating fully developed characters; students often do not. Their stories may be full of action and details, but they don't always draw the reader in because the characters are one-dimensional. We may be told what they look like and what they do, but we do not care sufficiently about them because we know nothing of what goes on inside their minds and hearts. Characters in students' stories rarely seem to struggle or change, usually because they have no goal; the story has no purpose but simply meanders along until *The End*.

To help students create fully developed characters in their realistic fiction, we focus a good deal of planning work on character, immersing students in it for two weeks before they move into actually developing their stories. It's a good starting point, because once a strong character is developed, the rest of the story falls into place more readily, for character motivation drives the plot. (Think of Charlotte's scheming in *Charlotte's Web*; without her determination and ingenuity, Wilbur's future would be bleak, and we would not have much of a story.)

We've also found that when students invest time in fully developing their characters before they draft a story, and when we encourage them to think about their big idea or message beforehand, a theme often naturally emerges from the events of the plot, as the character works out a problem in a way that reflects his or her beliefs. Consequently, the stories that result are richer and more satisfying than those written when we approached story-writing in a more traditional way. This chapter provides a framework for conducting a realistic fiction-writing cycle based on character.

Developing Character Traits: The First Step Toward Great Characters and Stories

When asked to describe their best friend, most people do not begin by listing physical traits, yet that is often how young writers describe their main characters. While physical appearance is important, it's personality that drives the action and gives the story emotional power. Or, as our students might say, "You need the inside to go along with the outside." We use picture books to show students just what we mean by the character's inner self.

Lesson on Character Traits: Inner and Outer

One of our favorite books to use for exploring character traits is *Amos & Boris* by William Steig, because the characters so clearly reveal their personalities through their actions. Amos, a mouse, goes on an ocean journey and is saved by Boris the whale; the two become great friends. Even though Amos is a wee little mouse, he is not diminutive in his actions, but mighty adventurous and resourceful. He goes against type, showing students the importance of knowing more than just superficial information about a character. (Other famous characters whose outer appearances don't match their inner selves are the Cowardly Lion, Bilbo Baggins, the Frog Prince, and the Beast from *Beauty and the Beast*.)

In the following lesson, Rosanne's students identify and categorize Amos's and Boris's character traits, discussing both their physical and personality traits. This activity helps students see that personality affects plot more than physical appearance does.

✓ Focus for Listening

Rosanne: While I read the story aloud, think about what we learn about Amos and Boris. What are they like? After the story, we will chart their character traits and see what we notice.

We brainstorm lists much like the one shown here.

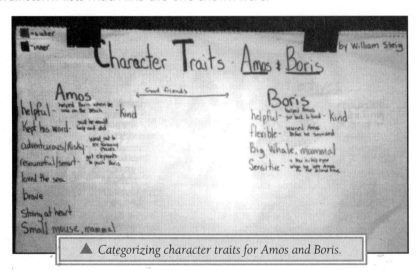

▲ *Categorizing character traits for Amos and Boris.*

Once students have finished brainstorming character traits for Amos and Boris—and have supported their ideas with examples from the text—we think about how we can categorize them. Students suggest category labels: physical/not physical, inner/outer, and personality/looks. We decide to use the terms *inner* and *outer*. We then rewrite the chart and color-code the traits as either inner or outer. This technique makes a dramatic point: all but one of the character traits for each character was inner, highlighting how important it is to develop a character's personality.

Rosanne: During writing time today, you will begin to create your own main character. Later on, these characters will become the stars of your stories. Keep in mind what we learned from our study of Amos and Boris: interesting characters have lots of inner traits that make up their personality and drive their actions. We also want to know what our characters look like, but remember how important the inner traits are. We want to look deeper than their physical characteristics. What are some ways you can begin organizing information about your character?

Lucy: Well, we could make two lists—inner and outer—and brainstorm traits for each category.

Adam: You could put your character's name in the middle of a web and do it that way.

Rosanne: Two good ideas. Anything else?

Marc: I think it'd be easier to just write about my character in sentences.

Rosanne: Okay, you can free-write too. So now you have three ways you can begin sorting information as you explore your character. We'll meet back here at the end of the period to discuss what we find.

✓ Sample Conference

While the students were working, Rosanne sat beside Amy, who often has difficulty getting started with her writing.

Rosanne: How's it going?

Amy: I don't know. It seems kind of hard.

Rosanne: What seems hard?

Amy: I'm having a hard time thinking about my character.

Rosanne: What would you like to know about this character?

Amy: Well, I know I want it to be a girl. I need to think about her personality.

Rosanne: One strategy writers use is to borrow character traits from people they know. Or you can borrow from other characters. Can you think of any characters or people that you like?

Amy: [Pause.] Oh yeah, Grace, you know, in *Amazing Grace*.

Rosanne: What about her?

Amy: She's a talented actress, and she won't take no for an answer. When they tell her she can't play Peter Pan, she proves them all wrong.

Rosanne: So what can you borrow from Grace for your character?

Amy: It's not that I want my character to be an actress, but I like how

Grace stood up for herself. That's what I want for my character. I want her to be like that, not let anyone boss her around.

Rosanne: That's a great start. I like that you were able to discover the traits behind Grace's actions in the story. Now think of some other characters or people that you can borrow from.

Facing a blank page is difficult for any writer, and many students have Amy's problem. We have an arsenal of specific strategies to offer students when they have trouble developing characters; see tip box at left.

After conferring with other students in the class, Rosanne checked with Amy to see how she was doing. She had brainstormed several personality traits and named her character, and was now working on a physical description in paragraph form. Rosanne asked her to share with the class; Amy agreed.

As students generate traits for their characters, they will inevitably create positive traits as well as flaws, and may even begin to see how these traits can lead to trouble—the plot of the story. This is precisely the point of beginning with a well-developed character—we want the stories students write to emerge naturally from the characters they create. If students do come up with story ideas at this point, we encourage them to write them in their notebooks so they are available when students begin drafting.

✓ Homework: Character Interviews

After the share, we suggest interviewing characters as a way to get to know them better, a strategy Nancie Atwell discusses in *In the Middle*. As a class, we generate interview questions that will reveal a character's personality. That night, students interview their future characters for homework, using the questions we made up in class. (See sample interview at right.) Many of the questions emerge from the literature discussions we have about characters throughout the year. We find that students are more prepared to think

Name	Date

Character Interview Questions

Use these questions to help you think about your character.
Write on the back or on another sheet of paper if you need more space.

What is your name and age? _____

What do you look like? _____

Where do you live? _____

What is your family background? _____

What do you like to do? _____

What is special about you? _____

What do you care about? _____

What do you fear? _____

What are your dreams? _____

How would a friend describe you? _____

You are the type of person who . . . ? _____

Who are the important people in your life? Why? _____

What are the important things in your life? Why? _____

What are the problems you are facing? _____

How will you change? *(Possibilities: get stronger, get a better self-image)* _____

What will you understand about yourself and your work at the end of your story?
(Possibility: the world is a harsh place) _____

about the characters they are developing once they have examined and discussed characters in books, and we encourage them to look closely at the characters in their independent reading. Thinking critically about all characters they encounter helps them to think more deeply about the characters they are creating as writers.

▲ *A student used interview questions to write her initial character description.*

Follow-up Activities: Lessons for Developing Character Traits

Over the course of two weeks studying character, offer students a variety of follow-up activities to give them more criteria for well-developed, memorable characters. Here's a sampling of some follow-up lessons we have used successfully.

Create a Class Character

Generate personality traits for a class character. Record the traits on chart paper and refer to it during discussions of character, thinking aloud as a class about that particular character's personality, motivations, feelings, etc. You can use this character to model how to answer the interview questions described above, and the class can practice placing the character in a variety of situations and seeing how the character acts.

Create Sample Scenarios

Give students sample situations and have them imagine how their characters would react. Placing a character in specific new contexts helps students refine traits and may give them ideas for their story line. The situations that we have found most helpful are those that could really happen to our students and thus their characters. Remember, we want our students writing stories about things they know and creating characters that they have

TIP BOX

Having students interview a well-known character from a picture book helps them become familiar with the kinds of attributes authors reveal about their characters.

We make sure students feel free to revise their characters as the story develops, ensuring that the character's motivation, development, and relationships are aligned, making the character and story believable.

access to. Having a 50 year-old FBI agent as a main character would not be ideal. However, having a nine year-old girl moving to a new town would be. Some situations we have used in the past include:

* What would your character do if his/her parents would not let him/her go to the movies because the theater was in a bad neighborhood?

* Your character is at recess with his/her friends and they start picking on a new kid in school. How would your character react?

* Your character was walking home from school and found a wallet with $2,000 in it. What would he/she do?

When students respond to these situations, they write in narrative form. They do not answer with one or two sentences. Sometimes these situations appear in their stories, or even become the main focus.

> Rosanne's class created a character, Timmy, and then placed him in a situation to see how he would react. This whole-class activity models the process each student will follow for their own realistic fiction pieces.

Explore Significant Detail

Help students understand the nature of significant, or telling, detail. This is extremely difficult for most young writers but is certainly worth exploring. In *Writing Fiction,* Janet Burroway tells us:

Specific, definite, concrete, particular details—these are the life of fiction. Details (as every good liar knows) are the stuff of persuasive-ness. Mary is sure that Ed forgot to pay the gas bill last Tuesday, but Ed says, "I know I went, because this old guy in a knit vest was in front of me in the line, and he went on and on about twin grand-daughters"—and it is hard to refute the knit vest and twins even if the furnace doesn't work.

Describe a Character Using the Five Senses

We have found that the best entry point for teaching about telling details is to have students describe their character using details that stir the five senses, for this takes them a long way in the direction of selecting charac-ter-revealing details. Says Janet Burroway, "A detail is 'definite' and 'con-crete' when it appeals to the senses. It should be seen, heard, smelled, tasted, or touched."

To have students generate sensory-rich details for their characters, ask or post questions such as:

* What does her voice sound like?

* Does he sing in the shower? Does she have a favorite perfume?

* Does the scent of apple pie remind him of someone?

* What is his favorite color?

* Does she like walking home from school in the rain, or hate it?

* What does he do with his hands when he's nervous?

* What does she look like when she's mad? happy? sad?

Now Make the Sensory Detail Significant

Once students have explored the sensory details, have them look at their work and circle those details that seem to matter. For example, a young writer might decide that the fact that the character responds to the scent of apple pie is more important than that his favorite color is blue, because the former detail adds to the mood and perhaps links to a plot line of a boy missing his grandmother. Again to quote Burroway, "A detail is concrete if it appeals to one of the five senses; it is significant if it also conveys an idea or a judgment or both." *The boy*

▲ *A student works on developing her character in her writer's notebook.*

Recommended READING

Character Motivations/ Development

To explore character motivation and development, try the following books:

OBVIOUS:
Amazing Grace by Mary Hoffman

Amos & Boris by William Steig

Brave Irene by William Steig

Strong to the Hoop by John Coy

Thank You Mr. Falker by Patricia Polacco

The Wednesday Surprise by Eve Bunting

SUBTLE:
An Angel for Solomon Singer by Cynthia Rylant

Coming Home by Floyd Cooper

The Memory Box by Mary Bahr

wore a blue shirt when he walked into the kitchen is concrete because we can see it. *The boy walked into the kitchen and stood still a moment with his eyes closed, inhaling the scent of the pie and imagining his grandmother's gnarled old hands* is concrete, and also significant, because it conveys an idea—an insight into the character, namely, that the character misses his grandmother.

Needless to say, exploring telling details is a subtle, sophisticated matter of craft, and young writers will only begin to get the gist of it. Professional writers struggle throughout their careers to nail the telling detail; plan to introduce the significant detail to students, celebrate it when you see it in their stories, but don't hold the bar too high. Consider students who include sensory-rich details successful!

Share Your Character With the Class

Share how you developed your own character, taking students through your writer's notebook and thinking aloud about how and what you did. It's particularly effective to copy the relevant pages from your notebook onto an overhead so students can see the entries you're talking about.

Character Motivation and Development

Once students are comfortable with their characters, we explore character motivations and development. In good stories, characters are driven toward an objective. The plot unfolds because of the character's search for what he or she wants or needs. It is difficult for the reader to become attached to characters, and feel for what they're going through, if their motivations are not clear. Characters begin to change and develop as a result of their journey to reach their goal. Unfortunately, in many student pieces the characters do not change or grow in any way, resulting in stories that do not engage the reader. The pieces are monotonous since the characters remain stagnant. Working on the character's motivation and development catapults students' writing to the next level.

Lesson on Motivation and Development: Making the Connection

To help students see the connection between a character's motivation and subsequent development, we use *An Angel for Solomon Singer* by Cynthia

Rylant. In this story, Solomon longs to feel at home and not so out of place. He has recently moved to New York City from Indiana and feels very lonely. One night he goes to a diner where a friendly waiter, unbeknownst to him, becomes the impetus for Solomon's change. The waiter, whose name is Angel, opens Solomon's eyes and heart, and New York begins to feel like home.

In this lesson, Maria helps her students discover Solomon's motivation, and see how it becomes the impetus for his growth. They use a chart to guide and organize their thinking.

✓ Focus for Listening

Maria: Today we will be looking at character motivation and development. While I read, keep the questions on the chart in mind; they should help to guide your thinking.

Character Motivation and Development

What is the main character's goal?	How does the main character achieve it?	How does the main character develop/change?	What events occur to help him/her?

TIP BOX

Writing with your students allows you to share your process with them. It also enables you to model each step along the way, taking them through your writer's notebook and demonstrating how to develop character traits or sequence a plot. So if you haven't done it before, give it a try with your next realistic fiction cycle!

✓ Discussion

Maria: [Reads book.] Okay, let's take another look at the chart. What was Solomon's goal/motivation?

Lena: Well, he wanted to go back to his home in Indiana.

Jim: I disagree. He wanted to feel like he was home. He didn't really like it in the city because it wasn't what he was used to.

Maria: Oh, so you're saying that you think Solomon's goal was not necessarily to live in Indiana but to find a home, a place that felt like home.

Jim: Yeah.

Maria: What does everyone else think about Solomon's goal?

Sara: When I think about it, it is more that he wants to feel at home, rather than actually go back to Indiana.

Lena: I think I agree with that now. That's what we should write on the chart for his goal, that he wants to feel like he belongs.

Maria: Okay. What do you think we should look at now?

Nancy: Well, we have to look to see if he achieves his goal. I think he did, because he's not lonely anymore. I don't remember the exact words; could you read that page again?

Maria: "Solomon Singer has found the place he loves and he doesn't feel lonely anymore . . ." This part?

Nancy: Yeah.

Maria: So what do you think?

Jim: That sure seems to say he feels like he belongs now.

Sara: He's not lonely anymore; he likes where he is. We can say he met his goal.

Lena: Yes.

Maria: All right. Now, how do you think he achieved his goal? And what happens to help him?

Frank: The waiter in the diner. He was so friendly and kept asking him to come back. Solomon felt welcomed.

Sara: At the café, he keeps going back and ordering his dreams up in his head.

Deshawn: And the cat. He has a cat in the end, and that makes him feel like he's home.

Lew: Yeah, and he really wasn't supposed to have it. But it didn't seem like he cared.

Maria: I'll write all that here. The waiter, ordering up dreams, and the cat. How do you think he changed/developed in order to achieve his goal? How was he different from the beginning to the end?

Frank: Well, I think he changes because he likes the city now and before he didn't.

Sara: And he also looks at things differently, like in the beginning he doesn't like the city lights, and in the end he sees them as stars. I think that's it; could you reread those parts?

Maria: In the beginning, "So much of Indiana was mixed into his blood that even now, fifty-odd years later, he could not give up being a boy in Indiana and at night he journeyed the streets, wishing they were fields, gazed at lighted windows, wishing they were stars, and listened to the voices of all who passed, wishing for the conversations of crickets." And in the end, "The lights in the buildings twinkled and shone like stars, and he thought them lovely. And the voices of all who passed sounded like the conversations of friendly crickets, and he felt friendly toward them."

Jonathan: Oh, wow, I didn't notice that before.

Liz: Yeah, neither did I. I think he sees the city differently at the end because of the change. Now that he feels he belongs there, he looks at it differently.

Maria: So he sees things differently at the end. I'm gonna write that here [points to third column].

Nancy: And also what Frank and Liz said, that he now feels like the city is home.

Maria: Good. Let me ask you, though: Do you think Solomon changed all of a sudden, at the very end?

Liz: No, I guess it was slowly.

Maria: Yes, slowly. This is an important idea to remember when you write your own stories. Characters change and develop in response to events and people—in Solomon's case, people's warmth—and they do so gradually. Solomon is able to feel at home in the city because he was open to the city's beauty and its people's kindness. If he hadn't been open to that, the story would have unfolded quite differently.

Maria and the class complete the chart. In pairs, the students look through the class picture books for character motivation/development and fill out the charts Maria provided, which they later shared. Students can then use these charts for their own stories, helping them to plan how their character will change during their story.

During the share, the students noticed that in *Brave Irene* by

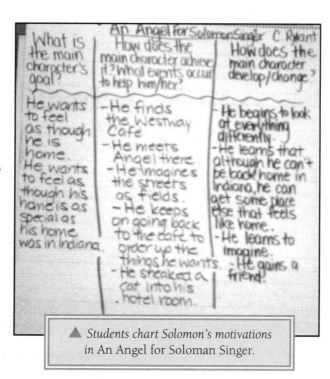

▲ *Students chart Solomon's motivations in* An Angel for Soloman Singer.

William Steig, Brave Irene's motivation was the main focus of the book; this led to a discussion of whether or not this occurred in other books. The students agreed that they could make the generalization that the character's motivation drives the plot in all books. We asked them to test this theory on their independent reading books and other stories to see if it holds up.

Homework

For homework the students developed possible motivations for their characters.

Eva Hoffmann   April 12, 2000
Lynn's motivation
Lynn is a person who is motivated through the story to do many different things, Although in the middle of the story she is not motivated due to the fact that she is only focused on believing that she is not a smart enough person to achieve her goals, the end has a lot of motivation. She wants to thank her best friend, Marjorie, for doing the right thing. She also wants to apologize to Marjorie because she was very rude and hadn't realized that her best friend was doing the right thing. She is also motivated to help her father in both the beginning and the end.

Francesca
Situation for my character
The situation I will try out is:
Daniella will try to be like everyone else. She is different because she has no mother or father, only an aunt or uncle. She gets teased for her American name in Italy although, her last name is of course Italian. Everyday her want for a better life becomes bigger and bigger until one day out of the blue tells her aunt and uncle that she wants a real mother and father.

▲ *Eva and Francesca's possible character motivations, which provided the basis for their stories.*

Peer Conferences: Aligning Character  Motivation/Development With Character Traits

The following day, Maria asked students to look closely at what they had done for homework. In peer conferences, students discussed whether or not they had succeeded in creating motivations and development for their characters that made sense. Partners decided whether the ideas were

TIP BOX

You can have discussions with students about why the character's motivation is so important to the story and what would happen if the motivation changed. It can be fun to have students change the character's motivation and then see what happens to the story.

Aligning Your Character's Motivation/Problem and Traits

Why does your character have the problem he or she does?

Is there something about his/her personality that causes/contributes to the problem?

What do you know about your character that will determine how he/she will react to the problem?

How will your character have to struggle to solve the problem?

Is the struggle realistic?

Will someone else help your character solve the problem?

How will facing the problem change your character?

convincing by looking at the character traits. While students were working, Maria pulled a small group together and created the following questions to help guide their thinking.

Character Relationships

Through our previous lessons on character, discussions on character relationships emerge. A character's relationships play a major role in how the character changes and grows throughout the book. Many characters gain strength or are inspired by other characters. Often another character is an obstacle. Additionally, the main character may be pushed toward his or her goal by the actions of other characters. These relationships move the story along and create tension that keeps the story interesting. Students need to realize that there is a reason why a specific character is in the story.

Even though the importance of character relationships appears in our discussions and in students' writing, we read picture books to enhance their understanding that a character is not isolated from the actions of other characters.

We use charts to demonstrate this concept. Some students use these charts to organize their own stories and thinking. Students can use the structure of the chart to examine how the character relationships in their own stories are working.

Minor Characters

We also introduce the idea of a minor character when discussing character relationships. These characters play small roles in the story and do not need to be fully developed. They often serve as stock characters and help move the plot along or serve as a contrast to the main character. For example, in a story about a junior high student trying to make the basketball team, the evil team captain could serve as the main obstacle and would not need to be developed as fully as the main character. Helping students differentiate between main and minor characters allows them to focus their attention on the character that needs to be fully drawn and just do a quick sketch of the others.

Using Graphic Organizers

With all this thinking and planning about character, motivation, plot, and character relationships, it's easy for students to become overwhelmed or

Recommended READING

Character Relationships

To help students understand character relationships, share the following titles:

Amos & Boris
by William Steig

Chicken Sunday
by Patricia Polacco

Fly Away Home
by Eve Bunting

Grandma According to Me
by C. Beil

Grandpa's Face
by Eloise Greenfield

In the Time of the Drum
by Kim Siegelson

My Mama Had a Dancing Heart
by Libba Moore Gray

Peach & Blue
by Sarah Kilborne

Sunshine Home
by Eve Bunting

Song and Dance Man
by Karen Ackerman

The Chalk Doll
by Charlotte Pomerante

The Memory Box
by Mary Bahr

The Memory Coat
by Elvira Woodruff

The Two of Them
by Aliki

The Wednesday Surprise
by Eve Bunting

Through Grandpa's Eyes
by Patricia MacLachlan

When I Go Camping with Grandma
by Marion Bauer

White Dynamite & Curly Kidd
by Bill Martin Jr.

confused. To help students organize their thinking, we provide graphic organizers and charts. These tools scaffold their ability to plan on their own, and over time students internalize the structures. Ultimately, they become flexible enough to design their own tools for the variety of writing purposes they encounter.

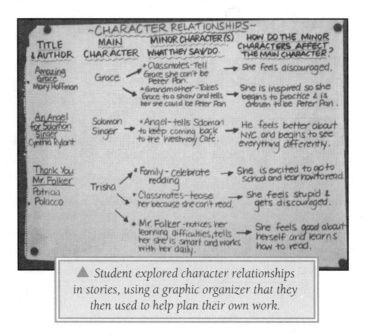

▲ *Student explored character relationships in stories, using a graphic organizer that they then used to help plan their own work.*

Introducing Big Idea

Discussing the difference between big idea, or theme, and plot throughout the year enables our students to create stories that carry a bigger idea or truth about human beings or society. After lessons on character traits and motivations, students are ready to think deeply about the theme at work in their stories.

Young readers often confuse big idea with plot. To clarify this for them, we explain that plot is the beginning, middle, and end of a story—how the story's events occur. The big idea has more to do with the meaning of the events—what the story says about a particular subject or topic.

Use Read-Alouds to Tease Apart Big Idea and Plot

If reading is making meaning, writing is creating meaning, and stories often express greater truths about human nature than do mere events in the plot. Early in the year, we spend a great deal of time discussing big ideas in the books we read, and establishing how a big idea is different from a plot. By the time we begin our realistic-fiction cycle, students have some experience with big idea. It's not until this time that we formally discuss big idea as it relates to writing. We now draw on all the work we've done in the reading workshop to strengthen what we're trying to do in the writing workshop.

Several weeks prior to beginning her realistic-fiction writing cycle, Maria reads *The Giving Tree* by Shel Silverstein aloud, focusing on the concept of big idea.

✓ Focus for Listening

Maria: Today we're going to read a book that many of you are already familiar with. For the most part, you know what this book is about. Authors usually have some big idea, or message, that they want us to hear. Shel Silverstein does in this story. As I'm reading, think about what that big idea might be, and think about how the events support the message. We'll chart everything when I'm done reading. You can use your literature notebooks to take notes.

Maria reads aloud the book.

✓ Discussion

Maria: Okay, let's start with what you think the plot was about.

Victor: Mostly it was about how this kid grows up and keeps on going back to take from the tree.

Lisa: Yeah, and the tree keeps on giving things to this man all the way up until the end.

Liz: But this guy doesn't really appreciate it, no matter how many times the tree gives him anything.

Maria: Would you say that the plot is this guy taking from the tree until the tree has nothing left to give?

Class nods and Maria writes that on the chart.

Maria: Now, the big idea makes a statement that's larger than the plot. So if you had to name the big idea in *The Giving Tree* in general terms—as an idea that goes beyond the events in the story—what would you say?

Cynthia: I guess it's that the tree loves the boy so much that he's willing to give him everything.

George: Even himself—by the end, he was just a stump. It's kinda horrible.

> ### Recommended READING
>
> **Theme, or Big Idea**
> These books have a strong theme:
> *Amazing Grace*
> by Mary Hoffman
> *Amos & Boris*
> by William Steig
> *Chrysanthemum*
> by Kevin Henkes
> *Fireflies*
> by Julie Brinckloe
> *Horton Hears a Who*
> by Dr. Seuss
> *I Have an Olive Tree*
> by Eve Bunting
> *I Wish I Were a Butterfly*
> by James Howe
> *Lilly's Purple Plastic Purse*
> by Kevin Henkes
> *My Little Island*
> by Fran Lessac
> *Odd Velvet*
> by Mary Whitcomb
> *Smoky Nights*
> by Eve Bunting
> *Sunshine Home*
> by Eve Bunting
> *The Big Box*
> by Toni Morrison
> *The Giving Tree*
> by Shel Silverstein
> *The Little Red Lighthouse & The Great Bridge*
> by H. Swift
> *The Memory Box*
> by Mary Bahr
> *When I Go Camping with Grandma*
> by Marion Bauer
> Patricia Polacco books

Vaughn: If you think about it, this kid or man was so selfish and the tree was so giving.

Anita: Yeah, it's kinda like the tree was the parent, and the kid was the child always depending on the parent.

Maria: Good. What underlying message was coming through the plot? What nugget of wisdom is the author trying to share with us?

Anita: I guess it would be love means giving up everything, all of yourself, for the one you love.

Maria: Wow. That's a pretty big message for such a small book, isn't it?

This read-aloud–based lesson using *The Giving Tree* is one among many. As we read picture books and novels throughout the year, we continually discuss theme and encourage students to weave this element into their own writing. We ask students to think about what big idea they'd like to express as they're creating their characters. Then, as they consider events and situations for their stories, their big idea can guide them to scenarios that will allow them to express their message.

Motivation—
In this realistic fiction story, Lynn's motivation is to pick her life up from the way that it had been before. She wants to repay Marjorie for all of the help that her best friend has given her, and apologize for not being thankful. She wants to help her mother, find her father, and become a regular kid again.

Big Idea.
There are quite a few big ideas in my story. The messages I want the reader to know is that you really have to believe in yourself, and you have to realize that although today you aren't thankful, tomorrow you may be. One of the main message in my story is that a true friend does what is best for you—which is not always what they want to do.

▲ *Eva outlines her character's motivation and thinks about her big idea; the two are clearly related.*

Big idea is a challenging concept for young writers to grasp and incorporate in their work, so if they're having difficulty with it at first, we sit with them and guide them to discover the big idea in their story. We might say to a student, "For your own writing, remember that the events or plot of your story should convey meaning beyond the mere series of actions. So as you write, think about the big idea you want to emerge from your work. Be aware of it as you go along, and nurture it as you write." Or, more specifically, if a student is writing a story about a young girl whose father isn't supporting her wish to join Little League, we will ask a question that nudges the writer to think about the larger meaning. What does this relationship say about parents and children? Is there an underlying message you think you're sending through your story, about how parents and children express their love for each other in spite of their differences?

We also find it helpful to look back on the charts that we have constructed over the year. We do this in order to show how events in a story get across the big idea, challenging ourselves to name the big ideas in the books that appear on the chart. For example, in *Amos & Boris* by William Steig, the big idea is that friendship can flourish between people with very little in common on the surface, and that these enduring friendships can be lifesaving.

We have found that after discussing big ideas and messages embedded in stories, our students' writing grows considerably. They begin to think deeply about the stories they write, looking for what they want to say about the world and giving their work meaning and purpose.

TIP BOX

Peer conferences are a great place for students to discuss theme and think about how it is working in their stories.

Synthesizing Our Planning: Bringing It Together

After the character and big idea lessons, students should have a solid idea of where their piece is going. They know their characters, their problems and motivations, and they've identified potential situations and events. Now we want students to organize their ideas, articulating specific events that will occur and move their stories along.

We have designed a graphic organizer that has been helpful for these purposes. We introduce the organizer by reading Patricia Polacco's *Chicken Sunday* and filling in the organizer with the class. We have an enlarged version or have drawn it onto our chart paper (or on an overhead transparency). Once students are familiar with the organizer, they can adapt it to help them structure their own stories.

Chicken Sunday is a poignant story about three children who show their love for their grandmother, Miss Eula Mae, by working and saving money to buy her a hat she had been admiring.

✓ Focus for Listening

Maria: *Chicken Sunday* by Patricia Polacco is a story that is organized in a way that I expect many of your stories might be. A problem is introduced and then the characters try a few different ways to solve the problem. You'll want your characters to make a few attempts before they solve their

TIP BOX

The graphic organizer we use for *Chicken Sunday* (see next page) helps students organize their own work as well. The boxes on the top show the events that introduce the problem. Point out to students that some stories jump right into the problem without any events leading up to it; they can consider this when planning their own stories. Also encourage them to adapt the organizer to fit their story; perhaps they will have two or four events leading up to the problem. This tool helps them think through their planning decisions.

problems, also. Otherwise, the story won't be very interesting. Notice the graphic organizer on this chart. While I'm reading the story, think about how we'll fill it in.

Maria leads a discussion reviewing the different components of the chart and then reads the book; she fills in the top three boxes with the events that lead up to the problem.

✓ Discussion

Maria: Now that we've identified the events leading up to the problem, let's continue filling in the chart. What's the main problem in the story? What are the characters striving toward? What is their goal? Why is it important to them?

Grace: They want to buy the grandmother a hat for Easter.

Jacob: And they don't have the money.

Marianne: And they have to make the money.

Maria: Then the problem is that they need to make money to buy Miss Eula a hat. I'll put that here [points to chart]. Now, how did the problem get solved? What did the characters do?

Carolyn: After they realized they didn't have enough money, they went to the owner of the hat shop to ask if he needed help. You know, they wanted to make some money.

Maria: Okay, is that the first attempt?

Class nods yes.

Maria: That would go here. Then what happened?

Keshawn: Well, the owner blamed them for throwing eggs and called Eula Mae. She made them apologize even though they didn't do it.

Shanta: But that's not another attempt.

Carolyn: Right. I'd say the next attempt is when they go back to the store with the decorated eggs. You know, to make a good impression, and then they ask him if he has any work for them. He says no.

Shanta: Yeah, I agree.

Keshawn: Me too.

Maria: So I'll put that here. Then what happens?

Jacob: He, the shop owner, suggests they sell the eggs. He volunteers his store.

Maria: Is that the third attempt? What happens next?

Erin: Well, they sell the eggs and have more than enough money to buy the hat.

Alex: Yeah, but the owner gives them the hat without making them pay. He knew what they were doing and said they were good kids.

Maria: Was the problem solved? Did they reach their goal?

Class nods yes.

Maria: Okay. I'll put what Alex said here.

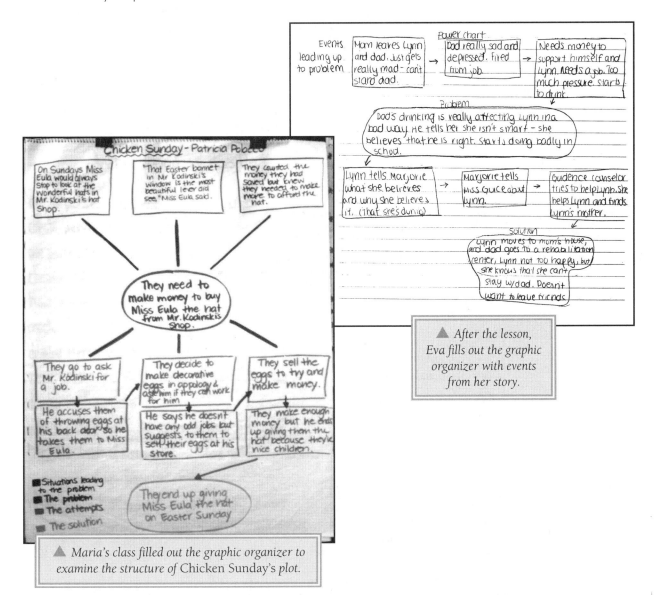

▲ *After the lesson, Eva fills out the graphic organizer with events from her story.*

▲ *Maria's class filled out the graphic organizer to examine the structure of Chicken Sunday's plot.*

Maria reviews the chart, pointing out that each attempt caused the characters to respond and therefore try the next attempt, demonstrating that the attempts are connected, not isolated.

Maria: For writing today, I want you to create a chart like this in your writer's notebook and use it to guide your planning. Remember that the attempts should be connected, as we saw in *Chicken Sunday*. There should be a cause and effect relationship. If you finish your chart in class, find a partner or me, and confer. Remind your conferring partner that each attempt needs to drive the next. Your homework tonight will be to complete the chart.

Maria circulates, trying to meet with as many students as possible to ensure that they will be ready to draft tomorrow or the next day. During share time, she asks students what they noticed as they used the chart. Did it help their thinking? Did it make gaps or inconsistencies clearer?

Sequencing Events

① Mom leaves dad b/c they get into a big fight. → ② Dad really depressed. can't eat or concentrate b/c he is really sad. → ③ Dad starts drinking heavily b/c he can't hold up his job

Mom - mad! Dad - depressed, upset. Lynn - Embarrassed b/c they fought, sad b/c dad is sad, and mad that mom left.

Dad gets kicked out of job b/c he can't concentrate.

Lynn worried about dad.

④ While he's drunk, dad tells Lynn that she isn't smart. Lynn believes it.

⑥ Marjorie tells Miss Guice, the psychologist.

⑤ Lynn tells Marjorie. Lynn trusts that she won't tell.

Lynn convinces herself that her father is right and starts to feel

Lynn mad! Won't talk to Marjorie.

Marjorie promises that she won't tell, but she really wants to tell.

helpless and dumb. Does bad in school b/c she thinks she's dumb.

⑦ Lynn has to go to Miss Guice, who slowly begins to help her and show Lynn that she really is smart

⑧ w/ Miss Guice, Lynn becomes a normal kid and starts doing well in school again.

At first, Lynn is very doubtful, but then she realizes that Miss Guice is helping her.

wants to find a way to thank Marjorie for helping her so much.

⑨ Miss Guice finds mom, and since Lynn's dad is drunk, Lynn moves to mom.
At first mad at father b/c he made her move away from friends. But then she realizes she loves her dad and is sad to leave friends.

▲ *Eva further adapts the graphic organizer for her own story, sequencing the events along with characters' responses and feelings.*

Follow-up

The following day Maria reads another picture book and fills in another chart to solidify the components and reinforce her expectations. She then meets with students to check their progress. If a student's chart is completed satisfactorily, he or she can begin drafting or assist classmates who are having some trouble fleshing out their ideas. Within two days, all students should be ready to draft their stories on loose-leaf paper. Here is more of Eva's planning work.

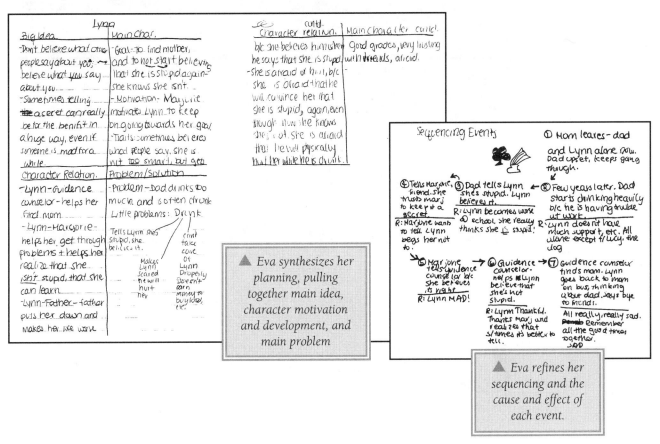

▲ Eva synthesizes her planning, pulling together main idea, character motivation and development, and main problem

▲ Eva refines her sequencing and the cause and effect of each event.

In this chapter we described the planning lessons we do with our students when we begin a realistic fiction cycle. After we have focused on character and explored big ideas, students come out of their writing notebooks and begin to draft their stories. The following chapters discuss revision strategies we work on with our students.

CHAPTER 6

▲ *Students study beginnings from various picture books.*

Writing Strong Beginnings and Endings

O nce students have drafted a narrative, we spend our writing workshop time exploring various revision strategies. We like to focus on beginnings and endings early in the term and revisit them throughout the year since students often neglect these important pieces of their writing. We've all read our share of "When I woke up this morning . . ." or "This report is about . . ." or read a promising story that ended abruptly. To avoid these common pitfalls, we've developed lessons that help students understand the importance of strong beginnings and endings and learn about various strategies writers use to create them.

Beginnings

Student writing pieces, both narrative and nonfiction, often begin with bland, unoriginal lines, usually because students need to put something on that piece of paper to get started. Anything is better than a blank page!

The problem is that they often neglect to go back to the uninspired beginning and rework it to draw the reader into their piece. When specific strategies writers use to create exciting beginnings are made explicit, students can move away from these boring leads. Picture books are an excellent source of compelling beginnings, and a picture book mini-inquiry is the perfect way to get students thinking about new and exciting ways to open their pieces.

Picture Book Mini-Inquiry to Study Beginnings

Before students publish their first piece of writing, we spend a few days gathering great beginnings and identifying the strategies we can use to create our own. To launch this mini-inquiry, we ask the students, in pairs, to spend 30 minutes looking through the class picture books to find beginnings that they like. The students divide a page from

▲ Student notebook page from beginnings mini-inquiry.

their literature notebook into three columns and label them "Title," "Beginning," and "Strategy Used." (See sample above.)

We ask them to keep the Strategy column blank since we will work on that column as a class. (We want everyone using a common language.) However, while the students are researching, we tell them to brainstorm possible names for the strategies they notice. Some strategies authors use to hook the reader include:

* engaging dialogue
* creating a mood
* starting with an astonishing fact
* describing a character's feelings
* using humor

* jumping into action
* asking a question
* describing a character
* describing the setting
* creating suspense

After about half an hour, we call the class together and chart what students found. The conversation may go something like this one from Maria's class.

✓ Discussion

Maria: Who wants to share one of the great beginnings they found? Gina?

Gina: We used *Two Bad Ants*: "The news traveled swiftly through the tunnels of the ant world. A scout had returned with a remarkable discovery—a beautiful sparkling crystal."

Maria: Why do you think this is a great beginning?

Sean: [Gina's partner] Well, it jumps right in.

Gabriel: Yeah, and you want to know what the crystal really is.

Maria: Okay, so Chris Van Allsburg got you interested because he started right into the story; he began with action. That's one of the strategies that authors use. He also mentions an enticing object—the beautiful crystal—which creates some suspense, another good strategy to hook your readers. Did anyone else find beginnings with those characteristics?

Laura: Yeah, we have one from *Gorky Rises* by William Steig. "As soon as his parents kissed him good-bye and left, Gorky set up his laboratory by the kitchen sink and got to work." So right away, we're wondering what he's going to work on.

TIP BOX

Continually read aloud leads from chapter books, nonfiction works, and newspaper and magazine articles. Encourage students to share leads from their independent reading and to bring in any interesting leads they notice.

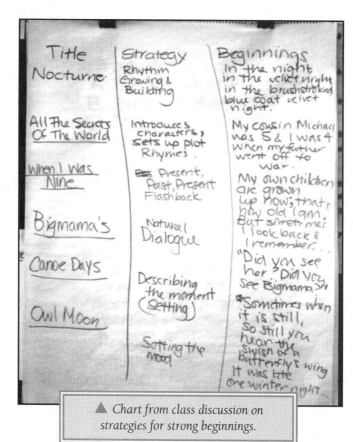

▲ *Chart from class discussion on strategies for strong beginnings.*

The class continues to share, discuss, and categorize interesting beginnings they found in their study.

If you lead the discussion this way, students actually categorize the different strategies on their own and begin to distinguish one strategy from another. Maria continued the discussion until the students had mentioned all of the strategies she had jotted in her notebook. If students do not mention all of these, she names them and has the class look for them for homework and continues the discussion the next day. Students then experiment with different beginnings in their own pieces.

✓ Conference

An individual conference is a great time to suggest that a student revisit his or her lead. In the conference that follows, Rosanne encourages Zak to work on the beginning of his piece because his original draft is very event driven: "This happened, then that happened, then that happened . . . ." The reader has no context for the action and feels no investment in the piece. Notice how our study of picture books enriches the discussion and provides Zak with ideas for revision.

▲ *The first draft introduction of Zak's "My Best Summer Ever."*

Rosanne: I read your piece last night, and it sounds like you had a great time on your vacation. You're very descriptive. Let's take a look at your lead. What were you trying to accomplish with it?

Zak: Well, I wanted people to be interested in my vacation.

Rosanne: And do you feel people will be interested after reading your first few lines?

Zak: [Rereads first line.] Maybe not. It tells that it was exciting and that I was scared, but there's nothing really there to show what was exciting or scary.

Rosanne: That's a good observation. What can you do about that?

Zak: I could show what was exciting and scary.

Rosanne: I like that idea. You could jump right into the action. The reader will figure out where you are.

Zak: Oh, you mean like in *Two Bad Ants?*

Rosanne: Yes, exactly. Come find me when you're finished; I want to take a look.

Zak went right to work and came back with two new first lines. They were a definite improvement. However, the rest of the piece remained just a retelling of what he did on his vacation, so the reader still felt little or no investment. Rosanne had another conference with him.

Rosanne: Wow! This first line is great. What is it that you really want the reader to get out of your piece? Why did you choose to share this particular story?

Zak: It was an exciting trip for me, so I guess I want them to feel that.

Rosanne: Okay, you want them to feel your excitement. Why don't I read this back to you and you tell me, as a reader, how it sounds. [Rosanne reads the piece to Zak.]

> *The water splashed over our boat, soaking us and almost capsizing us. This was just one of the adventures we went on in Niagara Falls. That was our jet boating trip down Niagara River. I was extremely nervous but when the announcer said they had never lost one person, we were a tiny bit relieved.*

Rosanne: So what do you think?

Zak: Well, it doesn't really sound exciting.

Rosanne: Okay. What do you think you could do to make it more exciting?

Zak: I could probably include more action instead of just one line.

Rosanne: Can you find a place where you could do that?

Zak: I could tell more about the boat ride. I really only have one sentence of action describing it, and it was really exciting. I can add more about that.

Rosanne: Good idea. You could also try another one of the strategies. Maybe dialogue, like in *The Seashore Book,* when the little boy asked his mother what the seashore was like.

Zak: Yeah, I think I'll try both and see which one I like better.

See the lead to Zak's final piece on the next page. What a difference!

As demonstrated through Zak's piece, the beginning of a story can make a big difference. Having a wealth of picture books to refer to helps us as teachers to suggest strategies that

> ### MY TRIP
> *"Dad, I'm freeeeeeeeezing!" I said, as the ice cold water poured over us. "We're going out of control!!" My dad said as the driver pulled amazing 360s and spun us like a salad being tossed! "We're going toooo fast! My brother said as we went over 70 miles per hour! Our driver did a cycle, <u>Wash, Spin and Dry</u>. As we crashed through the waves, my dad lost a bandanna in the confusion. That is besides the fact. It was the most exciting boat experience I've ever had.*

▲ *The lead to Zak's final draft, now titled "My Trip."*

may be appropriate for a particular piece; it also helps students see how a particular strategy works in a story of comparable length and scope to their own. It's as though each of the books they know is another teacher in the room, an expert they can turn to whenever they want help.

Throughout the year, we continue to look at beginnings, not only in picture books, but also in novels, short stories, articles, and nonfiction texts. We ask students to keep an eye out in their own reading and bring in samples they think are particularly strong. We keep adding to our class chart from all these sources, including student beginnings as well. Here's an effective student lead from Eva's realistic fiction piece. (Much of her planning work for this piece is presented in Chapter 5.)

> <u>My Realistic Fiction Piece</u>
>   Families aren't perfect. They never can be perfect, and they never will be. Least of all ours.
>   Mama and Papa never really got along- not as far as I can remember. They didn't quite fight like children would, I guess, but Mama seemed as if she spent her time looking for things that Papa did wrong- why, I never really knew. Mama always said that she hated Papa but I don't think she ever really meant that- she just said it. They wouldn't have gotten married if they never loved each other- there had to be at least a little while when they did love each other, right? Their arguments were never too bad- well, I guess that's what you would say. They slammed doors and yelled, glared with icy stares for a while afterwards. You might say it wasn't too bad. But for me it was pure torture. It was embarrassment. Why couldn"t they get along? I wondered. They were full grown adults! I wanted to scold them and put them up in their rooms, like a mother with two fighting children, but they were the parents, not me! For a while I was mad, angry, unhappy with them. I sulked and brooded, thinking about how unlucky I was. But then again, they weren't hurting me. Eventually I just calmed down. Of course I was still humiliated that they were fighting and all, but it could be worse, right?

Working on leads is another good opportunity to show students your writer's notebook and share your attempts at creating compelling beginnings. You can discuss why you tried a particular type of beginning for a particular piece and talk about why it worked or didn't work. This modeling and thinking aloud helps students when they turn to their own work.

Students at Work

Our work on strong beginnings carries over into all the writing students do, in all curriculum areas. Here's a sampling of openings from nonfiction and fiction pieces written by our students.

TIP BOX

If you do not have a lot of picture books for the inquiry, you can provide the students with beginnings you think are great and ask them to categorize the characteristics they have in common. Bring in leads from your own favorite fiction— adult and children's literature—and then, as a class, name the characteristics (strategies) you notice. You can still keep an ongoing chart throughout the year.

Imagine that it is January 20, 1961, and it is freezing cold outside, in Washington, D.C. You are out there, sitting in a folding chair surrounded by thousands of people. Everyone is looking up at the new president and listening to his inauguration speech. "And let every nation know, whether it wishes us well or ill, that we shall pay any price, bear any burden, meet any hardship, support any friend, oppose any foe to ensure the survival and success of liberty." As he speaks, you start to feel hope well up inside of you, a way you have not felt for a long while. You sit there, and think about how glad you are that this wonderful man will be in charge of the USA for the next four years. The guy is John Kennedy, the 35th president of the United States.

—by Casey, fifth grader, from a report on John F. Kennedy

"Many people think I am an average girl, and I guess I am. I am like other girls in lots of ways, and then I have special things that make me Margery, not Denise or Paula or Iris or Sara or anyone else but Margery." Margery wrote thoughtfully. "For example, my red curly hair. Some people think that having red hair is a disadvantage, but I like mine. It makes me my own person. I think red hair looks pretty good on me (not to be stuck up or anything), so when people tease me, who cares?"

Margery's teacher paused and read over Margery's shoulder and commented . . .

—by Katherine, fifth grader, realistic fiction piece

Endings

How a piece of writing ends can make or break it. It's the last impression the reader has of our idea, the last chance we have to persuade or inform or move them. We find that many of our students end their pieces—narratives and nonfiction—too abruptly, leaving the reader unsatisfied and with a negative feeling toward the entire piece. We stress the importance of creating an ending that offers a sense of closure, and we highlight several different kinds of endings to get them thinking. The endings we discuss with our students include:

* **Poignant Endings**—These endings evoke emotion through something the character has learned or felt.

* **Endings That Have a Message**—These endings teach a lesson or have a moral or big idea.

* **Restatement of Idea**—These endings summarize the events or facts from the text, adding the essence or insight gleaned through the

character's situations or the knowledge learned.

* **Endings That Leave the Reader Wondering**—The endings make readers wonder, *Well what happens now?* or, in nonfiction, provide additional questions for readers to think about.

* **Circular Endings**—These endings add a certain sense of closure. They allow you to revisit some beginning details that at first might have seemed inconsequential, but in fact are the threads that hold the story together.

* **Surprise Endings**—These endings are different from what the reader may have expected and thus motivate the reader to go back and find "the popcorn pieces left in the path" leading to the ending.

We often do the same kickoff lesson for endings as we do for beginnings—the mini-inquiry described on page 95—except that students are looking for and charting endings. We also focus on a few ending types as the need or interest arises.

TIP BOX

Even though our students are familiar with most of the picture books they use for the mini-inquiry, they often find it helpful to reread the entire book or skim it while doing this activity. It's a great idea to read short stories, articles, and nonfiction pieces while discussing great endings.

Sample Lesson on Circular Endings

The circular ending is easy to identify, so it's easy for students to emulate, making it a good place to start. It encourages students to look at their

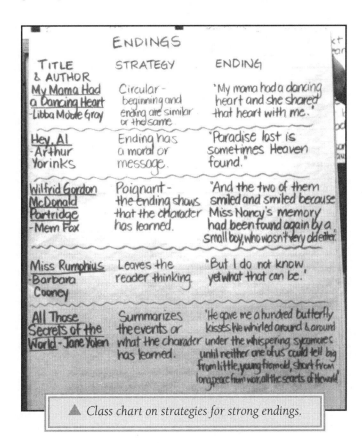

▲ *Class chart on strategies for strong endings.*

work as a whole and find some strand that can tie it together. They then weave that strand into the beginning and ending of their piece. Students can begin and end with the same description, feeling, telling detail, or spoken line, depending on what will work with their piece. Here's a sample discussion from a lesson on circular endings.

✔ Focus for Listening

Rosanne: As you know, we have been focusing on endings for the past few days, since many of you are working on that aspect of your writing pieces. We have scoured our picture books and come up with different kinds of endings and the different strategies one might use to create a satisfying ending. Today we're going to reread *My Mama Had a Dancing Heart* by Libba Moore Gray, and I'd like you to listen carefully for how she crafts her ending.

Rosanne reads the book.

✔ Discussion

Rosanne: So what do you think?

Karen: I think it's a circular ending because she begins and ends with the same line.

Kahan: I agree. The ending reminds you of the beginning, and makes it seem like you've come full circle.

Rosanne: And what do you think about that?

Mykela: I liked it.

Rosanne: Why?

Mykela: Because it goes along with the passing of time. Last time we talked about how time passes in the book—fall, winter, spring, summer. Well, next is fall, so the cycle continues. It's like Libba Moore Gray wanted to keep the cycle going.

Karen: Yeah, the circular ending is perfect for this story, since the story itself is about cycles.

Rosanne: Great connections. So think about the structure of your story and what kind of ending would work best with it. That's a good point to make. Anyone else?

Harrison: Well, I liked it because the girl became a dancer like her mother, and it seems like the last line might pertain to her, you know, the girl. Like maybe she has a dancing heart and she'll share it with her daughter.

Rosanne: I see. Yeah, that's a nice thought. Did anyone else find new meaning or more meaning in the same line from beginning to end?

Kahan: I appreciate and have a better feel for what the author means when she says "My mama had a dancing heart." When I hear it at the end, I picture all the things that happened in the book, and I actually see the dancing heart.

Rosanne: That's great. Anyone else?

The conversation continues, and Rosanne ends by having one of the students reiterate the different types of circular endings—same line, same place, same event, same feeling. Then she invites students to try out circular endings in their pieces.

Rosanne: Remember, just because you try this strategy out does not mean you have to use it. Some people may not even like circular endings. It is the author's choice. Also, if you feel like you're not ready to work on your ending then by all means, do not. Save this information for when you are ready.

Students got right to work. Following is an example from one student's final piece.

Lead to the story "Duane," by Lucy

"Daddy?" I said, answering the phone.

"Yes, sweetie, can I please talk to Mom?"

"Why, what's the matter? Where are you?"

"I'm at the vet, now can I please talk to Mom?"

"Is Duane all right?"

"No!" He broke into sobs.

Ending to the story "Duane"

"Daddy?" I said, answering the phone.

"Yes, sweetie, can I please talk to Mom?"

"Why, what's the matter?"

"We're getting the kittens today!"

Books to use for circular endings include: *On Call Back Mountain* by Eve Bunting, *Wilfred Gordon MacDonald Partridge* by Mem Fox, and *My Mama Had a Dancing Heart* by Libba Moore Gray.

✓ Try It Out

Once we have searched for satisfying endings, and have named the different strategies, we sometimes have students rewrite endings to our favorite picture books. Students love this assignment, and it affords them the opportunity to practice different types of endings.

Students at Work

The work we do with endings improves student writing in all the content areas, not just fiction. Below are some sample endings from research reports and a book review.

That's D-Day for you. Gruesome but needed. Strong but grueling. But it was worth it. Two years of planning was just enough for such a fight. It was the biggest invasion ever. You can't question why the Big Three would plan this so early and then use all their strategies and efforts in one month. It is what was needed. And what is needed, is what must be done.
> —by Richard, fourth grader, report on D-Day

I think the author's purpose in *Stuart Little* is that size doesn't matter, and Stuart was a human in the heart. And to him that is all that counts!!!
> —Margaret, fifth grader, book review

At her funeral everything came back. That walk in the park, this game of catch, even the way she walked. And I just sat there, watching and waiting. Realizing how much more we could have had. Together.
> —Natalie, sixth grader, memoir

The workshop time we spend on beginnings and endings helps students frame their pieces so the reader is drawn into them and finishes still thinking about them. We revisit beginnings and endings throughout the year in our writing workshop as part of the revision process. The next chapter covers another focus for revision: pacing and timing of events.

CHAPTER 7

▲ *Rosanne meets with two students to discuss pacing in a picture book.*

Pacing, Flashbacks, and Other Techniques of Timing

In our busy world, we are always racing against the clock, always juggling every minute of every hour. Despite our hectic pace—or perhaps because of it—humans seem to have a need to take time out to share funny, scary, or sad moments with a friend, relative, or anyone who is willing to listen. As we relive those moments, we know instinctively which parts to dwell upon—and those we can skip altogether—to make an entertaining story. Unfortunately, this winnowing process somehow becomes a challenge when writing. To help our students select relevant events and details, and spend the appropriate amount of time on them, we talk specifically about techniques writers can use to set a pace for their story that will keep the reader interested.

We address elements of time—including chronology, pacing, "hot spots," and flashbacks—during revision periods in our classrooms for both realistic-fiction and memoir-writing cycles. These elements of time can be addressed prior to drafting, but we have found these concepts most beneficial to students during and after the drafting process. The ideas become more meaningful, and the students can try them out immediately in an authentic way.

Chronological Time: Building Blocks of Story

Most students in the primary grades are able to write pieces that go, "this happened, and then this happened, and then . . . ." We call these bed-to-bed stories. We expect older students to write more sophisticated stories in which one event propels another. We want our students to use cause and effect when writing chronologically, selecting relevant events rather than recording everything.

Sample Lesson on Chronological Time

Rosanne begins a lesson on chronological time with *Music Over Manhattan* by Mark Karlins. She begins by discussing how stories are similar to buildings. The beginning of a story is like the foundation of a building. It sets the mood and anchors the story. The middle of a story is like the different levels, or floors, of a building. It is the main part of a story. And the end is like the top of a building. It is dependent on all the previous parts. It is the culmination. In stories that are chronological, time passes with each event building upon the last in "real time" to create the plot.

✓ Focus for Listening

Rosanne: While I'm reading, think about how the story is built. Notice how the beginning provides a foundation for the story and determines the initial course of events. Then consider how each event builds on the previous one and shapes the next. In your literature notebooks, sequence the story using the format in this chart, thinking about how and why one event drives the next. [Reads story.]

✓ Discussion

Rosanne: What happened first in the story?

Chris: Well, Bernie wasn't happy to go to the party.

Rosanne: Why?

Chris: Because his cousin was going to be there.

LeAnne: And his cousin was good at everything, and Bernie wasn't.

Rosanne: So Bernie was upset because he didn't feel smart or talented. I'll write that on the bottom block of our chart. This is the basis of the story. Then what happened?

Amanda: His uncle notices how sad he is and brings him to the roof to play the trumpet.

Rosanne: Okay. I'll write that on the next block. So because Bernie is upset, his uncle takes him to the roof. What happens there that moves the story along?

Mark: Bernie plays a few notes, and his uncle tells him he's got talent.

Rosanne: All right. What does the uncle do next?

Lee: He buys Bernie a trumpet.

Rosanne: Good. I'll write those events in the next block, that he played a few notes, his uncle thought he had talent, and so his uncle bought him a trumpet. We can see the connection between these blocks: Bernie's uncle learns about Bernie's talent because he was trying to help him when he was upset.

The conversation continued in the same fashion and we created a chart to summarize our discussion.

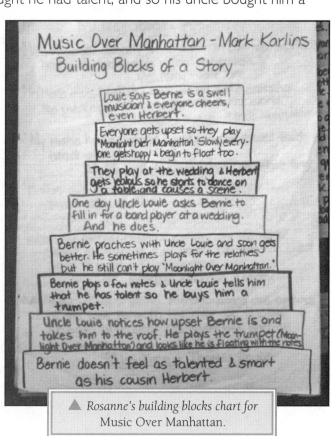

▲ *Rosanne's building blocks chart for* Music Over Manhattan.

✓ Try It Out

Rosanne then asks the class to sequence their own realistic fiction piece using the chart, helping them to see how cause and effect is working— or not working— in their pieces.

✓ Share

During share time, we ask students how using the building blocks chart helped their work. Here are a few comments from Rosanne's class.

▲ *Rosanne talks with students about cause and effect in their stories.*

LeAnne: I like it because it helped me focus on the cause and effect. I actually got rid of a few scenes because they didn't seem to help the story.

Chris: That happened for me, too. I had to cut one of my favorite sentences because it didn't say anything.

Lee: Well, I discovered that what I thought made sense really didn't. I'm going to have to rewrite one of my scenes so that the cause and effect is really clear.

Our discussion on chronological time takes about two days. There are some students, however, who still have difficulty grasping the concept and relating it to their own stories. We usually have individual content conferences or smaller group lessons to review this process.

Snapshot

Snapshot picture books are very different from chronological picture books. In snapshot stories, the events are connected by a theme or focus, rather than time or cause and effect. These types of picture books are not that common, and this strategy is appropriate for only certain types of narratives, so we usually reserve the strategy for a piece that calls for it, teaching it during a conference rather than to a whole class.

Student Conference

Maria noticed that Cary's story seemed to ramble, and it was dry even though the topic—his mother—was emotional and significant to him. Maria decided to help Cary focus on the most important events in his memoir—the ones he felt most attached to—instead of writing about everything he could think of. That way, he could create a more engaging and satisfying piece. Maria sat with Cary, a student in a 3-4 bridge class, to help him move his memoir along.

Maria: What are you writing about, Cary?

Cary: My mom.

Maria: Why did you choose to write about her?

Cary: Well, because she is important to me.

Maria: Then why do you seem frustrated?

Cary: Because it seems to go on forever. I don't really feel like I know where it begins and ends.

Maria: I can see what you mean. *When I Was Nine* by James Stevenson is a picture book that I think will be helpful. Why don't you read it tonight and see where it takes you with your writing?

The next day Maria touched base with Cary; this is a bit of that conversation.

Maria: How did your writing go last night? Did the book help?

Cary: Yeah. At first I wasn't sure about how it was going to help, so I had to read it again. But then I got an idea, and saw how it could help me.

Maria: Oh, so what did you do with your writing?

Cary: In the book the man is thinking about all the things he did as a kid, you know, when he was nine. Each page is about a new thing, so I tried that for my paper last night.

Maria and Cary take a look at his revised writing.

When My Mom Is Away

When my Mom is away, I get school lunch instead of home lunch.

When my Mom is away, my baby-sitter picks me up from the Y instead of my parents.

When my Mom is away, dinner is the same every night instead of a varied dinner.

When my Mom is away, my friend's dad takes me to school.

When my Mom is away, I am with my babysitter more than with my Dad during the week.

When my Mom is away, I play at my friend's house a lot more.

When my Mom is away, I get to go to basketball practice every Saturday with my Dad instead of every other Saturday.

And the best part about it is
She brings me back
a
present.

It is evident in this final piece that Cary was able to find a common thread running through the seemingly unrelated ideas from his beginning drafts. The strand Cary discovered was how he feels when his working mother is away on business. The suggestion Maria gave Cary—to take home and look deeply at *When I Was Nine*—provided Cary with a model for creating an emotionally powerful piece. We often refer to specific picture books when conferring with students and urge them to take the books home to steep themselves in the work.

Pacing

Pacing a story can be very difficult for young writers. Many times the beginnings of their stories are well developed and the endings are rushed. Other times, students give equal time to the important and unimportant events. A great story depends a lot on how well the plot unfolds. Pacing events so that the most important parts get full play—and the parts that do not develop plot, character, or setting are omitted—is key, and helps keep the reader interested. We ensure that our students are very familiar with the books we use to teach pacing, so they can focus on the pacing and not the particular events.

Sample Lesson: When to Slow Down

This is a lesson from Maria's class, where they discussed the pacing of their stories.

✓ Introduction

Maria: Has anyone ever told you to pace yourself when you're running a race or playing soccer?

Jess: Sure.

Maria: Why?

Jess: Well, you've got to make sure you have enough energy to finish the race, or the game.

Alex: In soccer, sometimes you slow down, so when it's your time to go after the ball, you're ready.

Maria: So what do you think it would mean to pace a story?

Lynn: I guess it would be to make sure you've got enough energy left for the end.

Jess: Yeah. The high point is near the end a lot of times, and sometimes I run out of time before I get to it.

Keisha: I think it also means to be ready for the important parts, and put a lot of effort in them. Like you do in soccer when it's your turn at the ball.

Maria: You're making great connections. I don't know about you, but I often have a hard time pacing myself, both in sports and in writing.

Kylie: Yeah.

Maria: It helps me to think about when I tell a story to a friend at lunch or on the phone. Then I automatically know which parts are important, which parts to put my effort on. I choose the details and events that will enhance my story, and I leave out those that are not relevant or are common sense. For instance, I wouldn't have to tell you how I got dressed that morning unless it's going to come up again later on in my story.

It is the same when you write a story. The parts that we want the reader to respond and connect to need to be well written, with a large portion of the story devoted to those parts. For instance: If I were telling you a story about the first time I ran the NYC Marathon, I might focus on how nervous I was, and about the last mile of the race, instead of giving you a blow-by-blow of all 26 miles. That would not be too interesting. However, if I focus on the last mile or two, when I make the turn into Central Park, knowing there are only two miles left, and all these strangers are cheering me on and giving me strength—that will make for an interesting story.

✓ Focus for Listening

Maria: While I read this story, *Midnight in the Mountains* by Julie Lawson, keep in mind which parts span a few pages and which parts have been left out entirely. Fold your paper down the middle and title the left side as "Parts Developed" and the other side "Parts Omitted." Remember that it is going to be easier to write about the parts developed; however, try to notice which unimportant parts the author has left out.

Maria reads aloud slowly, allowing enough time for the students to jot down their notes and to think about which parts have been omitted.

✓ Discussion

Maria: Let's start with the easier part. Which events did the author spend more time on? How did she show you, the reader, that this was an important part?

Lynn: She spent more time on the actual day's events.

Maria: Okay. Let's try to be more specific.

Anya: In the very beginning, when she is too excited to fall asleep, she thinks about her day. She starts by saying that she remembers doing the snow angels and how her dog Trouble's angel looked like a snowman.

Maria: Great. Is there something there that Julie could have mentioned but decided not to?

▲ *Students discuss pacing in
self-selected picture books.*

John: She never mentioned their ride there or even why it's her first night in the mountains. She just jumped in.

Tina: I agree. You kind of know she's just looking back on all the best parts of the day.

Maria: Right, so where is the next part where the author spends more time?

Douglas: When they're walking in the snow, and they see ice crystals, and their mom told them they would get frostbite.

Max: And when they got back to the house, the father played music on the icicles.

Maria: Were there any parts where the writer chose to leave something out?

Max: She didn't write everything they did—just the interesting things.

Maria: Right! What happened next?

Lara: Well, she wrote about the frozen creek, but she skipped a description about lunch.

John: That's because it has nothing to do with the mountains.

Maria: Right, that part wasn't important to the story. It's a book about the mountains, so their lunch isn't really relevant. Is there anything else?

Matthew: She spent a few pages describing the creek, and explaining how they went on the dogsleds, and how she thinks of the wolves when she hears sounds at night.

Douglas: Yeah, and she skipped everything from the dogsled to the night, when she was supposed to be sleeping.

Maria: How do these choices about what to include and what to leave out affect the story?

Anya: The story would have been much duller with all those details. This way, you stay focused on what it's like in the mountains—what you do, what it looks like, how it feels—which is the whole point of the story anyway.

Maria: Right. So when making these decisions, it's important to know what your point is. Think about this in relation to your own writing.

 ## Try It Out

Maria: During writing today, go back to your story and find the parts that are not necessary, that don't do a job in your story. Put a single line through them. You might find them more important later, so do not cross them out completely. Find and circle the parts that are crucial to your story, the parts that divulge feeling, character, etc. Then take those parts and list the important information you will need to expose that event entirely to the reader. For example, if my story was about how my mother and I really didn't get along, how the relationship with my mother changed, and how we learned to accept each other in the end, I may want to focus in on one of our fights. In my first draft I just mentioned the fight, but I think I need to slow down so the reader can get a real sense of the tension between me and my mother. If I were to do this, I would write "Event—Argument with mom" on the top of my page. Then I would brainstorm what I wanted to include in the story about the fight. Feelings, reactions, thoughts. Things like that.

Maria thought aloud, modeling for the students how to complete the exercise, and came up with the following chart.

Event - Argument with mom

She barged into my bedroom in the morning.

I was startled and looked up, rubbing my eyes and jumping out of bed.

I thought to myself—Now what? She won't even let me sleep late on a Saturday.

I could tell she was angry. She was doing that thing with her hands. Pulling at the sides of her pants, like she has an itch that won't go away. And that face. The pursed lips, slanted eyebrows, like on one of those cartoons. I almost expect steam to come out of her ears.

She asked what time I came in last night.

I mumbled the answer under my breath as I left the bedroom.

I knew how she hated it when I ignored her questions and didn't speak directly to her.

"When I ask you a question I expect you to answer it!" she screeched.

Maria then asked the students to try it out with their own stories, remembering to include as many details as they could come up with. The chart that Maria created in front of the class will remain up for the students to refer to.

Knowing when to omit certain uneventful parts and how to draw out crucial parts takes a lot of revision and sharing. We have students commenting on one another's work at this stage, and individual conferences are imperative.

Hot Spots

Pacing a story keeps the plot going strong and keeps the reader engaged. Writers control how quickly the events in their story move; they can slow down time depending on how important a particular moment is to the plot. Although it may take a few seconds for a car accident to actually occur, those few seconds might be crucial to your story and take up two pages. We call the parts that need to be stretched out *hot spots*, a term Ralph Fletcher uses in *Craft Lessons*. Hot spots often occur at the climax of the story, or where the problem is introduced. Hot spots are parts that show a character's feelings and thoughts, or smaller details that add action and description to a story.

Creating a Hot Spot

This lesson took place in Maria's class during a realistic-fiction study and after her pacing lesson. She uses a nonfiction book, *Home Run* by Robert Burleigh. It is Babe Ruth's life story and is a great book to use since it covers his whole life yet includes a hot spot.

✓ Focus for Listening

Maria: We've read this book before, and today I'd like you to focus your listening on the part you feel Robert Burleigh emphasized the most, where he slowed down his story. On the top of a clean page in your literature notebook, write the part you think is the hot spot, the part he slowed down. On the rest of the page, write down all the details he uses that slow the part down and make it memorable.
Maria reads the story slowly to allow students enough time to take notes.

✓ Discussion

Maria: All right, what parts do you notice were stressed and slowed down?

Lynn: Definitely the part where he was hitting the home run.

Maria: Why do you think that part was slowed down?

Lynn: Well, it's really the most important part of the story. I mean, that's what Babe Ruth was known for—hitting home runs—so it makes sense to spend a lot of time describing it.

Maria: Okay. How does he slow it down and make us feel this part is important?

Hot Spots—most important event
of a story/writing piece. A part that is
slowed down for a reader

Up At Bat

Slowly. Rotate. Powerfully.
Gone. —one word sentences
slow the spot down.

Home run. Home Run.
going. going. —repeating
sentences, phrases or words.

The fans crane their necks to follow.
slows it down by adding a picture
to your mind.

Babe Ruth's feelings are expressed.
"The feeling that is like no feeling at all."
You are introduced to his thoughts and
feelings which slows it down.

Mentions, "Going, going," 2 paragraphs/pages
later "Gone."
Although a home run happens in a few
seconds, Burleigh writes about what is
happening in these few seconds.

▲ *Class chart on hot spots in* Home Run.

Seth: He describes every move Babe Ruth makes, and all his thoughts and the actual hit are filled with details.

Martin: Yeah, even the sentences are different lengths.

Maria: What do you mean by that?

Martin: I think the sentences are sometimes shorter to stress that the author wants you to read this part slower. Lots of them are only one line long, and each one starts on a new line. That makes you slow down.

LeAnn: Yeah. I wrote something down about that. "Powerfully" is one sentence, on a line all by itself.

Maria: He spends about eight pages on this one event that takes a few seconds in real time. Why don't we chart the little details he uses. I'll read it again. [Reads selection.]

Maria's class charts the details from the passage and continues discussing how Burleigh slowed down time in this excerpt.

Book Excerpt:
from *Home Run*

Babe understands this feeling.
He does not know when or where.
But he waits for it.
He wants it.
Again.
And again.
He watches the pitcher lean.
Rotate.
Rock-back and forth.
The leg wheels out.
The arm whips over the head.
Babe narrows his hunter-like gaze
and strides into the pitch
that is now only a tiny speck of whirling whiteness.
This time.
He swings big.
His bat comes down and around.
Powerfully.
He swings "through the ball."
Always "through the ball."
There.
There it is.
The feeling that it's like no feeling at all!

The ball cracks off the bat.
It soars far up in the air
As it passes first base.
Going, going.
The fans crane their necks to follow.
But Babe already knows.
The perfectness.
The feeling.
The boy-fire inside the body of a man.
He moves down the line.
Slowly.
He squints.
He watches the ball disappear
in a distant blaze of white shirts and blurred faces.
Home run.
Home run.
Gone.
He trots with short steps.
Across the loose dirt of the infield.
Over the soft hardness of the bases
beneath his spiked shoes.
Under the roar of cheering voices
That falls on him like warm rain.
He waves his cap to the huge calling-out.
He loves this moment.
He is theirs.
They are his.

He is the Babe
And he has changed baseball
Forever.

For the rest of writing time, the students brainstormed about their hot spots and listed details under the hot spot title, just like the chart from the *Home Run* discussion. That night for homework, they were responsible for writing the hot spot using the listed details.

> Hot Spot   Lynn
>
> One night Papa came home drunk, as usual—there was almost never a night that he was sober. Usually he left me alone when he was drunk—he just muttered to himself. But this particular day Lynn was in the kitchen getting a drink of water when Papa came home. She had been thinking that it was really that her dad was "better" than her mom, she meant, he didn't leave her, her mom did. It may not have been his fault that he drank, maybe it was the stress of taking care of a child and his work. He came in staggering and she saw that his eyes were a bit bloodshot around the edges. He spoke, and when he did, his voice was not steady like a regular voice. He mumbled, and got louder. He was just talking non-sense, Lynn thought. But he pulled her over with a sharp jerk and looked her in the eyes. Hair hung in his face and he had a drunk sort of appearance. He started by saying that Lynn didn't know anything, she was stupid he said. He told her how she didn't know anything, and although Lynn knew Papa was drunk, he said it so much like he meant it and said it so viciously that Lynn began to think as he released her from his grasp. She walked into her bedroom-living room and unfolded her sheet from the couch. Teary as she might, Lynn could not manage to finally go to bed for quite a while. She tucked her knees up by her chin and began to wonder. Was she really right? Could it be true? Kids had called her stupid before, Lynn realized when she had gotten mad at the kids who teased her. Now the kids either left her alone—they just minded her business because she didn't bother them. But could it be true? The more she thought about it, the more possible it seemed to be.

▲ *This is the hot spot Eva added to her piece on Lynn.*

A lesson on hot spots is important in any narrative cycle. It helps students cut from and add to their stories and memoirs, highlighting the significant parts. It's helpful to model writing a hot spot from an entry in your writer's notebook. Simply choose an entry with an event that could be expanded upon. Read the entry aloud, and then on chart paper or the overhead, expand the event into a hot spot. Sharing hot spots in small groups and in conferences helps writers decide if a hot spot should be slowed down even more. We usually spend about a week on polishing these parts and getting them to appear to the reader as if they are the climax, or most important part, of the story.

Flashbacks

A flashback is an effective way to introduce a significant incident that occurred before the main action of the narrative. Every story has a story that precedes it, and using flashbacks is a great way for a writer to briefly bring the past into the present and illuminate the reasons behind a character's feelings or actions. Stories can begin with a flashback, or they may contain several throughout. When students understand the concept of flashbacks, and can incorporate them into their writing, they have another tool at their disposal to create effective narratives.

Lesson on Flashbacks

Rosanne read *Miss Rumphius* by Barbara Cooney to her class. Most of the story is based on a flashback that divulges the Lupine Lady's past. Rosanne discussed with her class how the author chose to present a lot of the character's past through flashbacks. She then asked the students to search the picture books in the class library for flashbacks and note the words and phrases the author used to signal that a flashback was coming. The following day they brainstormed a list to follow when using flashbacks in their own writing.

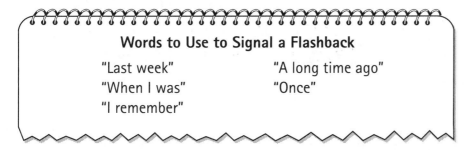

Words to Use to Signal a Flashback

"Last week"   "A long time ago"

"When I was"   "Once"

"I remember"

Rosanne then modeled how to write a flashback, drawing on entries from her writer's notebook and using the words generated by the class.

Although we have zeroed in on using picture books to teach specific elements of time, we cannot stress enough the importance of introducing a variety of texts to your students, discussing regularly how time is handled in every piece of writing they explore. Remember, the more good writing students are exposed to, the more able they are to emulate it.

CHAPTER 8

▲ *Students study dialogue in their favorite picture books.*

Using Monologue and Dialogue

> "Miss," Marcus yells from behind, and the ball bangs off the rim.
> I feel everyone's eyes on me and want to crawl off the court.
> "Go strong to the hoop," says Nate.
> "We gotta have those," says Zo.
> I know. I shouldn't be out here if I miss a shot like that.

This excerpt from *Strong to the Hoop* by John Coy illustrates the effective use of both interior monologue and authentic dialogue, techniques writers use to provide insight into their characters and move the plot along. Our students often struggle to bring their characters to life and show their characters' motivations; we've found that teaching interior monologue and authentic dialogue helps students create engaging characters and develop their plots without depending solely on narration.

Interior Monologue

Interior monologue is a window on characters' thoughts. It allows us to hear what they're thinking in their own words, which helps readers feel connected to and care about the characters. In our classrooms, we address interior monologue during revision times of narrative writing cycles.

Sample Lesson on Interior Monologue

For our first lesson on interior monologue, we like to use *Strong to the Hoop*. John Coy immediately brings readers into the main character's world by opening a window into his thoughts.

✔ Introduction

Rosanne: As I've been reading your stories, I often wonder what the character is thinking. When I've mentioned this, the author can immediately tell me exactly how the character is feeling. I think that since most of you know your characters so well, you feel that the reader does too. But readers only knows what we put on the paper, so you've got to let them "listen in" on what your characters are thinking during crucial parts of a story. This technique is called interior monologue.

✔ Focus for Listening

Rosanne: Today I will read *Strong to the Hoop* by John Coy. You all have typed versions of the story in front of you. While I'm reading, underline or highlight the parts where you notice interior monologue, where you can hear a character's thoughts.

Rosanne reads story.

✔ Discussion

Rosanne: So, what did you notice?

Jack: On the very first page James says he wishes he was bigger.

Rosanne: Right. And what did you learn about James from that?

Jack: Well, we learned that he really liked basketball and wanted to be bigger so he could play with his brother and his friends.

Rosanne: Good. Anyone else notice interior monologue?

Stephanie: Well, when he's playing there is a lot.

Tim: Yeah, like when he comments to himself about the other players. When he says he wants Marcus to shut up and play, he doesn't really say it. He just thinks it.

Rosanne: What did we learn about James from that?

Recommended READING

Books to Use:
I Know a Lady
by Patricia MacLachlan
Earrings
by Judith Viorst
Strong to the Hoop
by John Coy
The Ghost Eye Tree
by Bill Martin Jr.
The Memory Box
by Mary Bahr
Most "Alexander Books"
by Judith Viorst

Jessica: Well, that he wasn't going to take it from Marcus anymore. He seems like a very determined person.

Rosanne: I think so too. What do you think all the interior monologue added to the story?

Billy: Without it, the story would have been boring.

Jasmine: Yeah, it would just be like a retelling of a basketball game. You know—he dribbled, he shot, we scored, blah, blah, blah.

Tim: Like a sports commentary. I like it the way it is. You feel for James a lot more. I mean you really want him to beat Marcus.

✓ Trying It Out

Rosanne: Let's try adding interior monologue to our stories today. Choose a really important moment in your story and write some interior monologue. You may want to do it in a few spots. Let's brainstorm some possible places you might include interior monologue.

The class brainstormed the following chart.

> *Possible Places to Use Interior Monologue in Your Stories*
> *When your character . . .*
>   *first meets another character*   *has something important happen (happy, sad)*
>   *has to make a decision*   *is confused*
>   *is mad at another character*

✓ Share

Cary read aloud what he added to his piece during share time.

> "I think it would be more fun just to stay down here, it's not like there's nothing to do around this neighborhood," Kyle told them in a panicked tone.
>
> "Kyle, let's just go," Tom said, sounding annoyed.
>
> What should I do? Go with my friend and disobey my Mom, or listen to what my Mom said and not go with my friends? What are the chances of my Mom finding out that I went uptown? But what happens if she asks my friends what we did? They won't know not to tell her that we went uptown. If my Mom asks, I'll just quickly answer for them.
>
> "All right, I'll come with you," Kyle said in half-satisfied fashion.
>
> —by Cary, 5th grader

Cary used interior monologue to let his readers in on the conflict Kyle was feeling, adding depth to Cary's piece.

Students At Work

Here is an example of interior monologue from one student's realistic-fiction piece.

> When we got to the plane, the first thing we saw was passenger seating. The seats looked comfortable; they had lots of padding. There was another thing I liked about the plane, it was air-conditioned. The pilot also explained to me that if the plane is going to crash, everyone grabs a parachute and jumps off the plane landing safely on the ground. He showed me a video of people parachuting and I thought it looked like fun. The more I saw the less afraid I was. After the visit on the plane I felt like an idiot about my fear. I said to myself, How can anyone be afraid of planes, they're comfortable and safe. That trip seemed like the last straw between me and my fear of planes.
>
> —by Adam, 5th grader

You will be amazed at how quickly students can incorporate this element into their writing and at how much depth and interest it adds to their stories.

Authentic Dialogue

Students naturally include dialogue in their narratives. It makes the reading easier by providing breaks in the writing, it reveals a great deal about the character, and it brings the reader closer to understanding and connecting to characters. A difficulty many students face with dialogue is making it believable. People from different parts of town, the country, and the world speak in different ways and with personal variations. To effectively use dialogue, writers need to ensure it sounds authentic—that it reflects the character's background, geography, and personality.

Sample Lesson on Authentic Dialogue

We address authentic dialogue after students have written their first drafts. In the following lesson, Maria uses *White Dynamite & Curley Kidd* by Bill Martin Jr. and John Archambault.

✓ Introduction

Maria: Who knows what *dialogue* is?

Manny: It's when there is talking in a story.

Maria: Right. So what do you think *authentic dialogue* is?

No responses.

Maria: Well, let's figure it out. If I were from England and I said, "Mum, are we having biscuits for supper?" that would be authentic dialogue.

David: Oh, I get it. It's when people talk differently or when they have different accents.

Focus for Listening

Maria: Right. Authentic dialogue is when a writer writes the way a character would actually speak, including the slang and chopped up words. As I read aloud, tune your listening in on the way each character speaks in *White Dynamite & Curley Kidd* by Bill Martin and John Archambault.

Maria reads the story, having practiced a few times to make sure she is familiar with the conversations beforehand since the way she reads the text is important.

Discussion

Maria: Let's list the words that sounded like someone was actually saying them.

The class charts words that sounded like someone was talking. The list includes yep, actin', ol', goin' ta?, *and* plum dumb.

Maria: What did you notice about the dialogue?

Anya: Well, they never wrote, "he said" or "she said." They just wrote what the characters said.

George: I like that because it sounded like a father and a kid talking without any interruptions.

Maria: Right. The authors made it flow like an actual conversation would. Why do you think its works so well in this book?

Manny: Because the kid talks differently than the dad. They each have such distinct personalities and ways of talking, so it's easy to tell who's speaking.

Maria: Exactly.

Maria then asks students to spend the next 15-20 minutes adding picture books with examples of authentic dialogue to a special basket they can turn to when they need models for their work. The more examples they have to read and listen to, the easier it will be to read and listen to the dialogue in their own stories.

✓ Homework

For homework, we asked students to eavesdrop on an actual conversation and record it word for word. This activity makes students aware of the differences in the ways people speak and helps them think about how their characters should sound. The following day during our share time, we read bits of the conversations.

Follow-up

During writing workshop, we ask students to polish the dialogue in their own writing pieces. For most writers, the changes they need to make become more obvious when their pieces are read aloud to them. This is when peer conferences become especially helpful.

Following is an example of authentic dialogue from Adam's realistic-fiction story about parents deciding to take a trip to Disneyland in spite of their son's fear of flying.

> "Yeah, that would be great. There's lots of things to see and visit over there."
> "Yeah, but there's one problem—Adam's fear of planes."
> "I think it's time he grows up. I mean why should we suffer over something like that?"
> "Very true."
> "So then it's done. No more changes."
> "Absolutely."

Interior monologue and authentic dialogue help students bring their characters' voices into the stories, letting readers hear them firsthand. Focusing on these elements attunes students' ears to the language around them, which enhances their appreciation of language and enriches their writing.

Final Reflections

We breathe a sigh of relief knowing that this book is complete, but we also feel a bit apprehensive since it only represents part of our journey. The lessons and stories found in these pages highlight where we are now in our use of picture books and teaching of writing, but every year we glean new insights that enable us to improve our practice. We hope you use this book as a resource and as a diving board from which to plunge into your own unique interpretation of what we've modeled.

Recommended Picture Books by Author

Ackerman, Karen. *Song & Dance Man*. New York: Alfred A Knopf, 1988.

Aliki. *The Two of Them*. New York: Mulberry Books, 1979.

Altman, L.J. *Amelia's Road*. New York: Lee & Low Books, 1993.

Bahr, Mary. *The Memory Box*. Illinois: Albert Whitman & Company, 1992.

Barbour, Karen. *Little Nino's Pizzeria*. New York: Harcourt Brace & Company, 1987.

Bauer, Marion. *When I Go Camping with Grandma*. New York: Bridge Water Paperback, 1995.

Baylor, Byrd. *I'm In Charge of Celebrations*. New York: Alladin Paperbacks, 1986.

Bedard, Michael. *Emily*. New York: Doubleday, 1992.

Beil, C. *Grandma According to Me*. New York: Dell, 1992.

Brinckloe, Julie. *Fireflies*. New York: Macmillan, 1995.

Bunting, Eve. *Fly Away Home*. New York: Clarion Books, 1991.

　　—*I Have an Olive Tree*. New York: HarperCollins, 1999.

　　—*Secret Place*. New York: Clarion Books, 1996.

　　—*Smoky Night*. New York: Harcourt Brace & Company, 1995.

　　—*Sunshine Home*. New York: Clarion Books, 1994.

　　—*Wednesday Surprise*. Boston: Houghton Mifflin, 1989.

Burleigh, Robert. *Home Run*. New York: Harcourt Brace & Company, 1998.

Burmingham, John. *Cloudland*. New York: Crown Publishers, 1996.

Caines, Jeannette. *Just Us Women*. New York: HarperCollins, 1984.

Cherry, Lynne. *The Kapok Tree*. New York: Harcourt Brace & Company, 1990.

　　—*The River Ran Wild*. New York: Harcourt Brace & Company, 1992.

Cooney, Barabara. *Elenor*. New York: Puffin, 1996.

　　—*Miss Rumphius*. New York: Puffin, 1982.

　　—*Roxaboxen*. New York: Lothrop, Lee & Shepard Books, 1991.

Cooper, Floyd. *Coming Home*. Massachusetts: Silver Burdett Ginn, 1994.

Coy, John. *Strong to the Hoop*. New York: Lee & Low Books, 1999.

Dragonwagon, Crescent. *Home Place*. New York: Macmillan, 1990.

Fox, Mem. *Koalo Lou*. Melbourne: Ian Drake Ford Publishing, 1988.

　　—*Wilfrid Gordon McDonald Partridge*. New York: Kane/Miller, 1985.

Gray, Libba M. *My Mama Had a Dancing Heart*. New York: Orchard Books, 1995.

Greenfield, Eloise. *Daydreamers*. New York: Puffin Pied Piper, 1981.

　　—*Grandpa's Face*. New York: The Putnam & Grosset Group, 1988.

　　—*Grandma's Joy*. New York: Penguin Putnam, 1980.

Hall, Donald. *Ox Cart Man*. New York: Puffin, 1979.

Hazen, Barabara. *Tight Times*. New York: Puffin Books, 1979.

Henkes, Kevin. *Chrysanthemum*. New York: Greenwillow Books, 1991.

　　—*Lilly's Purple Plastic Purse*. New York: Greenwillow Books, 1996.

Hoffman, Mary. *Amazing Grace*. New York: Dial Books for Young Readers, 1991.

Honda, Tetsuya. *Wild Horse Winter*. San Fransico: Chronicle Books, 1992.

Houston, Gloria. *My Great Aunt Arizona*. New York: Harper Trophy, 1992.

Howell, Will C. *I Call It Sky*. New York: Walker & Company, 1999.

Jones, R.C. *Mathew & Tilly*. New York: Penquin Group, 1991.

Karlins, Mark. *Music Over Manhattan*. New York: Yearling Book, 1998.

Kilborne, Sarah. *Peach & Blue*. New York: Alfred A. Knopf, 1994.

Lawson, Julie. *Midnight in the Mountains*. Washington: Orca Books, 1998.

Lessac, Fran. *My Little Island*. New York: Harper Trophy, 1985.

Locker, Thomas. *Water Dance*. New York: Harcourt Brace & Company, 1997.

　　—*Sky Tree*. New York: HarperCollins, 1995.

MacLachlan, Patricia. *All the Places to Love*. New York: HarperCollins, 1994.

—*Through Grandpa's Eyes*. New York: HarperCollins, 1983.

—*What You Know First*. New York: HarperCollins, 1995.

Martin, Bill Jr. *Knots on a Counting Rope*. New York: Henry Holt & Company, 1966.

—*The Ghost Eye Tree*. New York: Henry Holt & Co, 1985.

—*White Dynamite & Curley Kidd*. New York: Henry Holt & Company, 1986.

McDonald, Megan. *My House Has Stars*. New York: Orchard Books, 1996.

McCloskey, Robert. *One Morning in Maine*. New York: Viking Press, 1952.

McKissack, Patricia. *Flossie & the Fox*. New York: Scholastic, 1986.

Morrison, Toni. *The Big Box*. New York: Hyperion Books for Children, 1999.

Myers, Walter D. *Harlem*. New York, Scholastic, 1997.

Nolen, Jerdine. *In My Momma's Kitchen*. New York: Lothrop, Lee & Shepard Books, 1999.

Numeroff, L. *If You Give a Mouse a Cookie*. New York: HarperCollins, 1985.

—*If You Give a Moose a Muffin*. New York: HarperCollins, 1991.

Oughton, J. *How the Stars Fell From the Sky*. Boston: Houghton Mifflin, 1992.

Paulsen, Gary. *Dogteam*. New York: Bantam Doubleday, 1993.

Pinkney, Andrea D. *Bill Pickett: Rodeo-Ridin' Cowboy*. New York: Harcourt Brace & Company, 1996.

—*Duke Ellington*. New York: Hyperion Books for Children, 1998.

Polacco, Patricia. *Chicken Sunday*. New York: Philomel Books, 1992.

—*Lubba & The Wren*. New York: Philomel Books, 1999.

—*Mrs. Katz & Tush*. New York: Bantum Doubleday, 1992.

—*Thank You Mr. Falker*. New York: Philomel Books, 1998.

—*The Keeping Quilt*. New York: Simon & Schuster, 1988.

Pomerante, Charlotte. *The Chalk Doll*. New York: HarperCollins, 1989.

Posey, Lee. *Night Rabbits*. Atlanta: Peachtree, 1999.

Quattlebaum, Mary. *Aunt Ceecee, Aunt Belle & Mama's Surprise*. New York: Doubleday, 1999.

Rylant, Cynthia. *An Angel for Solomon Singer*. New York: Orchard Books, 1992.

—*The Whales*. New York: Scholastic, 1996.

—*When I Was Young in the Mountains*. New York: Aladdin Books, 1991.

—*When the Relatives Came*. New York: Macmillan, 1985.

SanSouci, Daniel. *North Country Night*. New York: Bantam Doubleday Dell Books, 1990.

Schertle, Alice. *Down the Road*. New York: Harcourt Brace & Company, 1995.

Schotter, Roni. *Nothing Ever Happens on 90th Street*. New York: Orchard Books, 1997.

Schwartz, Ellen. *Mr. Belinsky's Bagels*. Massachusetts: Talewinds, 1998.

Sceiszka, Jon. *The Frog Prince Continued*. New York: Puffin Books, 1991.

—*The True Story of the Three Little Pigs*. New York: Puffin Books, 1989.

Sharmat, Marjorie. *Gila Monsters Meet You at the Airport*. New York: Macmillan, 1980.

Shanley, Mary K. *The Memory Box*. Iowa: Sta-Kris, 1996.

Sharp, N.L. *Today I'm Going Fishing with My Dad*. Pennsylvania: Boyds Mills Press, 1993.

Siebert, Diane. *Mojave*. New York: HarperCollins, 1998.

Siegelson, Kim. *In the Time of the Drum*. New York: Simon & Schuster, 1999.

Silverstein, Shel. *The Giving Tree*. New York: HarperCollins, 1964.

Steig, William. *Solomon & The Rusty Nail*. New York: Farrar, Straus and Giroux, 1985.

—*Amos & Boris*. New York: HarperCollins, 1971.

—*Brave Irene*. New York: Sunburst Books, 1986.

—*Shrek*. New York: HarperCollins, 1990.

—*Gorky Rises*. New York: HarperCollins, 1980.

Steptoe, John. *Stevie*. New York: HarperCollins, 1969.

Stevenson, John. *When I Was Nine*. New York: Greenwillow Books, 1986.

Stewart, Sarah. *The Gardner*. New York: Straus Giroux, 1997.

Stock, Catherine. *Island Summer*. New York: Lothrop, Lee & Shepard Books, 1999.

Swift, H. *The Little Red Light House & the Big Bridge*. New York: Harcourt Brace & Company, 1942.

Trivizas, Eugene. *The Three Little Wolves and the Big Bad Pig*. New York: Margaret K. McElderry Books, 1993.

Van Allsburg, Chris. *Polar Express*. Boston: Houghton Mifflin, 1985.

—*Jumanji*. Boston: Houghton Mifflin, 1981.

—*Just a Dream*. Boston: Houghton Mifflin, 1990.

—*Two Bad Ants*. Boston: Houghton Mifflin, 1988.

Van Leeuwen, J. *Emma Bean*. New York: Dial Books, 1993.

Voirst, Judith. *Earrings*. New York: Aladdin Paperbacks, 1990.

—*Alexander & the Terrible, Horrible, No Good, Very Bad Day*. New York: Antheneum Books for Young Readers, 1972.

—*Alexander, Who Used to Be Rich Last Sunday*. New York: Antheneum Books for Young Readers, 1998.

—*Alexander Who's Not*. New York: Antheneum Books for Young Readers, 1995.

Whitcomb, Mary. *Odd Velvet*. San Francisco: Chronicle Books, 1998.

Wild, Margaret. *Let the Celebrations BEGIN!* New York: Orchard Books, 1991.

Woodruff, Elvira. *The Memory Coat*. New York: Scholastic, 1999.

Wright, Courtni. *Journey to Freedom*. New York: Holiday House, 1994.

Wyeth, Sharon. *Always My Dad*. New York: Alfred A. Knopf, 1995.

Yashima, T. *Crow Boy*. New York: Penguin Group, 1955.

Yolen Jane. *Piggins & Picnic with Piggins*. New York: Harcourt Brace & Company, 1987.

—*Letting Swift River Go*. New York: Little, Brown & Company, 1992.

—*All Those Secrets of the World*. New York: Little, Brown & Co, 1991.

—*Owl Moon*. New York: Philomel Books, 1987.

Yorinks, Arthur. *Hey Al*. Toronto: Collins Publishers, 1986.

—*Louis the Fish*. New York: Farrar, Straus & Giroux, 1986.

Zolotow, Charlotte. *When the Wind Stops*. New York: HarperCollins, 1995.

—*I Know a Lady*. New York: Mulberry Books, 1992.

—*The Seashore Book*. New York: HarperCollins, 1992.

—*The Storm Book*. New York: HarperCollins, 1980.

Professional Resources

Anderson, Carl. *How's It Going?* New Hampshire: Heinemann, 2000.

Atwell, Nancie. *In the Middle*. New Hampshire: Heinemann, 1998.

Beck, Isabel, Margaret Mckeown, Rebecca Hamilton, and Linda Kucan. *Questioning the Author*. Delaware: International Reading Association, 1997.

Burroway, Janet. *Writing Fiction*. New York: HarperCollins, 1996.

Benedict, Susan and Lenore Carlisle, Eds. *Beyond Words: Picture Books for Older Readers and Writers*. New Hampshire: Heinemann, 1992.

Calkins, Lucy, *The Art of Teaching Writing*. New Hampshire: Heinemann, 1994.

Culham, Ruth. *Picture Books: An Annotated Bibliography with Activities for Teaching Writing*. Portland, Oregon: Northwest Regional Educational Laboratory, 1998.

Finn, Perdita. *Teaching Memoir Writing*. New York: Scholastic, 1999.

Fletcher, Ralph. *Craft Lessons*. Maine: Stenhouse, 1998.

—*A Writer's Notebook: Unlocking the Writer Within You*. New York: Avon Books, 1996.

—*What a Writer Needs*. New Hampshire: Heinemann, 1993.

Heard, Georgia. *Writing Toward Home*. New Hampshire: Heinemann, 1995.

Hindley, Joanne. *In the Company of Children*. Maine: Stenhouse, 1996.

Murray, Donald. *Crafting a Life in Essay, Story, Poem*. New Hampshire: Heinemann, 1996.

Ray, Katie Wood. *Wondrous Words*. USA: National Council of Teachers of English, 1999.

Zinsser, William. *Inventing the Truth: The Art and Craft of Memoir*. New York: Houghton Mifflin, 1995.